200 Knitted Blocks

200 Knitted Blocks

traditional and contemporary designs to mix and match

JAN EATON

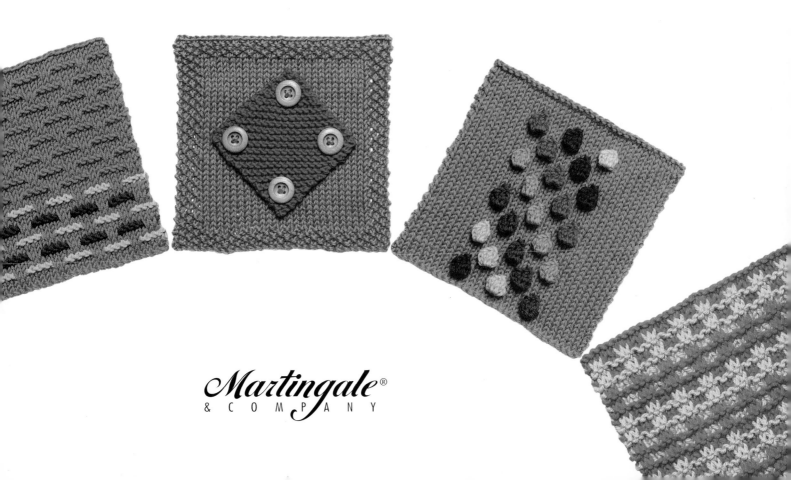

Martingale®
& C O M P A N Y

A QUARTO BOOK

First published in 2005 by
Martingale & Company
20205 144th Avenue NE
Woodinville, WA 98072-8478
www.martingale-pub.com

ISBN 1-56477-596-8

Library of Congress Cataloguing-in-
Publication data is available.

QUAR.ABT

Conceived, designed, and produced by
Quarto Publishing plc
The Old Brewery
6 Blundell Street
London N7 9BH

Project Editor: Jo Fisher
Art Editor and Designer: Elizabeth Healey
Assistant Art Director: Penny Cobb
Copy Editor: Fiona Corbridge
Photographer: Colin Bowling
Illustrator: Coral Mula and Jenny Dooge
Proofreader: Jan Eaton
Indexer: Pamela Ellis

Art Director: Moira Clinch
Publisher: Paul Carslake

Color separation by Universal Graphics
   Pte Ltd, Singapore
Printed by SNP Leefung Printers Ltd, China

10 9 8 7 6 5 4 3 2 1

Contents

Introduction

How to use this book

CHAPTER 1
Mix and Match   11

Using color and texture   14

Planning your designs   16

Mix and match designs:

Heart's Delight   18

Bobble Fantasy   19

Blue Geometric   20

Modern Times   21

Merry-Go-Round   22

Edwardian Counterpane   23

Bright and Bold   24

Nocturne   25

Buttoned Pillow   26

Holiday Pillow   26

Baby Lace   27

CHAPTER 2
Block Directory   28

1 Speckle   30

2 Offset   30

3 Double Eyelets   31

4 Threaded Ribbons   31

5 Mini Stripes   32

6 Lace Chevrons   32

7 Target   33

8 Little Blocks   33

9 Pinstripes   34

10 Horizontal Ridges   34

11 Ritzy   35

12 Surface Cables   35

13 Ribby   36

14 Troika   36

15 Twilight   37

16 Mirror Image   37

17 Reversed Heart   38

18 Flowing Pinks   38

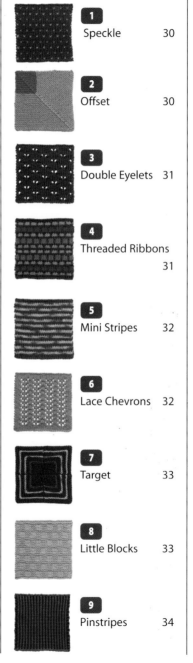

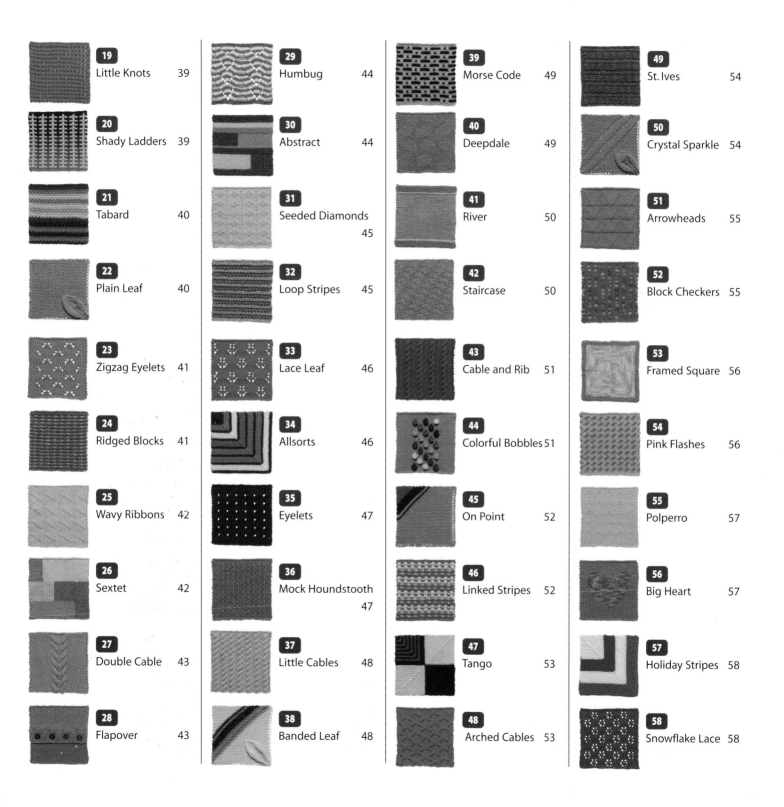

19 Little Knots 39

20 Shady Ladders 39

21 Tabard 40

22 Plain Leaf 40

23 Zigzag Eyelets 41

24 Ridged Blocks 41

25 Wavy Ribbons 42

26 Sextet 42

27 Double Cable 43

28 Flapover 43

29 Humbug 44

30 Abstract 44

31 Seeded Diamonds 45

32 Loop Stripes 45

33 Lace Leaf 46

34 Allsorts 46

35 Eyelets 47

36 Mock Houndstooth 47

37 Little Cables 48

38 Banded Leaf 48

39 Morse Code 49

40 Deepdale 49

41 River 50

42 Staircase 50

43 Cable and Rib 51

44 Colorful Bobbles 51

45 On Point 52

46 Linked Stripes 52

47 Tango 53

48 Arched Cables 53

49 St. Ives 54

50 Crystal Sparkle 54

51 Arrowheads 55

52 Block Checkers 55

53 Framed Square 56

54 Pink Flashes 56

55 Polperro 57

56 Big Heart 57

57 Holiday Stripes 58

58 Snowflake Lace 58

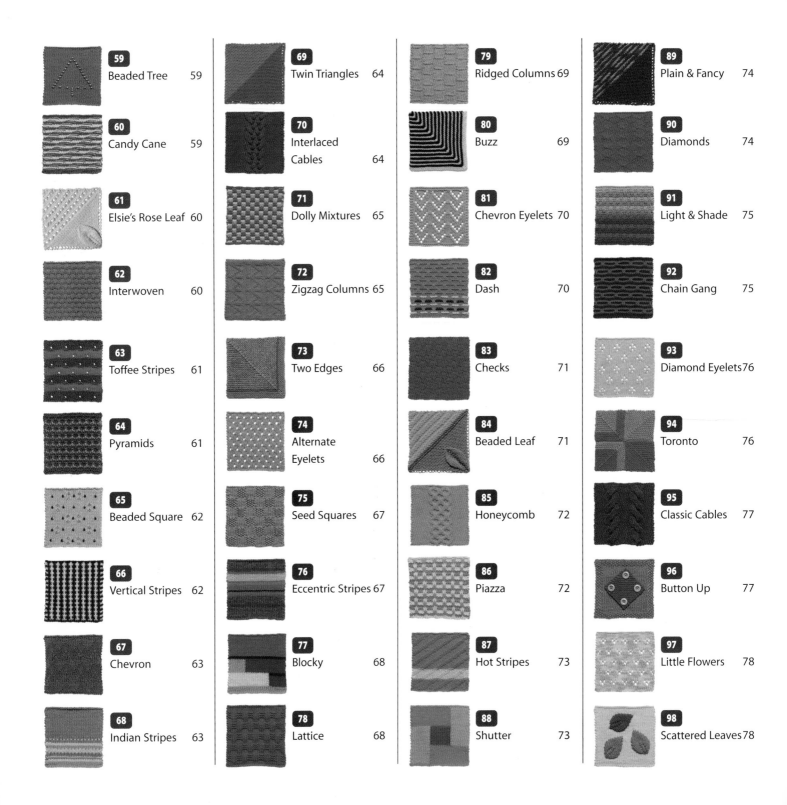

59 Beaded Tree 59

60 Candy Cane 59

61 Elsie's Rose Leaf 60

62 Interwoven 60

63 Toffee Stripes 61

64 Pyramids 61

65 Beaded Square 62

66 Vertical Stripes 62

67 Chevron 63

68 Indian Stripes 63

69 Twin Triangles 64

70 Interlaced Cables 64

71 Dolly Mixtures 65

72 Zigzag Columns 65

73 Two Edges 66

74 Alternate Eyelets 66

75 Seed Squares 67

76 Eccentric Stripes 67

77 Blocky 68

78 Lattice 68

79 Ridged Columns 69

80 Buzz 69

81 Chevron Eyelets 70

82 Dash 70

83 Checks 71

84 Beaded Leaf 71

85 Honeycomb 72

86 Piazza 72

87 Hot Stripes 73

88 Shutter 73

89 Plain & Fancy 74

90 Diamonds 74

91 Light & Shade 75

92 Chain Gang 75

93 Diamond Eyelets 76

94 Toronto 76

95 Classic Cables 77

96 Button Up 77

97 Little Flowers 78

98 Scattered Leaves 78

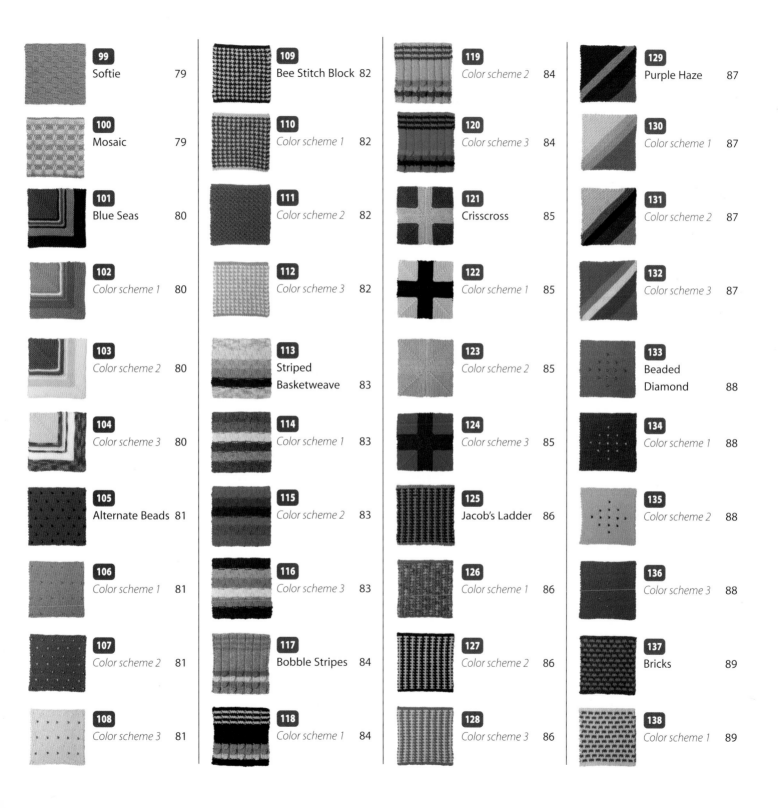

99 Softie 79

100 Mosaic 79

101 Blue Seas 80

102 Color scheme 1 80

103 Color scheme 2 80

104 Color scheme 3 80

105 Alternate Beads 81

106 Color scheme 1 81

107 Color scheme 2 81

108 Color scheme 3 81

109 Bee Stitch Block 82

110 Color scheme 1 82

111 Color scheme 2 82

112 Color scheme 3 82

113 Striped Basketweave 83

114 Color scheme 1 83

115 Color scheme 2 83

116 Color scheme 3 83

117 Bobble Stripes 84

118 Color scheme 1 84

119 Color scheme 2 84

120 Color scheme 3 84

121 Crisscross 85

122 Color scheme 1 85

123 Color scheme 2 85

124 Color scheme 3 85

125 Jacob's Ladder 86

126 Color scheme 1 86

127 Color scheme 2 86

128 Color scheme 3 86

129 Purple Haze 87

130 Color scheme 1 87

131 Color scheme 2 87

132 Color scheme 3 87

133 Beaded Diamond 88

134 Color scheme 1 88

135 Color scheme 2 88

136 Color scheme 3 88

137 Bricks 89

138 Color scheme 1 89

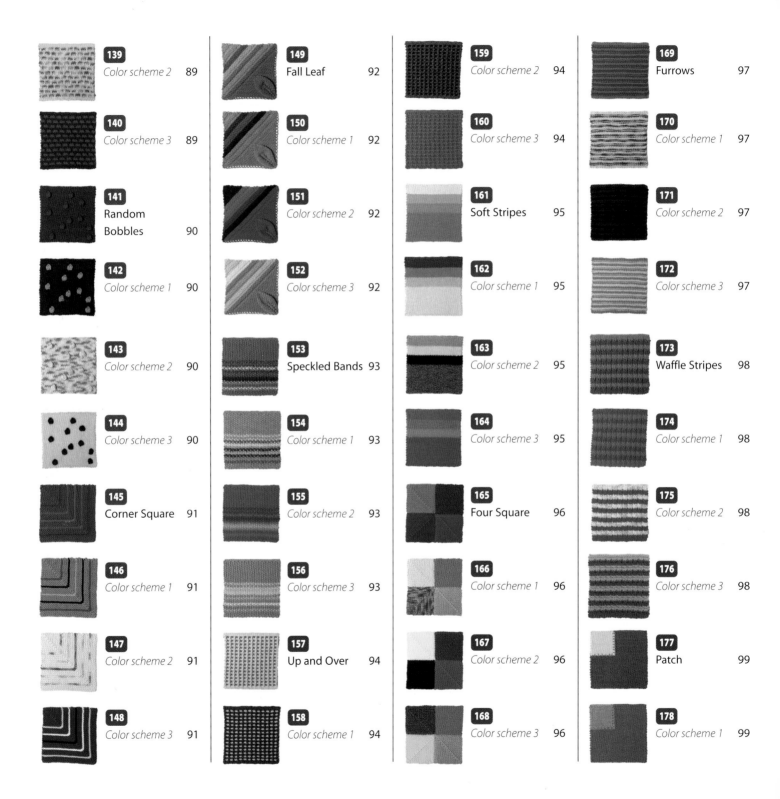

139 Color scheme 2   89

140 Color scheme 3   89

141 Random Bobbles   90

142 Color scheme 1   90

143 Color scheme 2   90

144 Color scheme 3   90

145 Corner Square   91

146 Color scheme 1   91

147 Color scheme 2   91

148 Color scheme 3   91

149 Fall Leaf   92

150 Color scheme 1   92

151 Color scheme 2   92

152 Color scheme 3   92

153 Speckled Bands   93

154 Color scheme 1   93

155 Color scheme 2   93

156 Color scheme 3   93

157 Up and Over   94

158 Color scheme 1   94

159 Color scheme 2   94

160 Color scheme 3   94

161 Soft Stripes   95

162 Color scheme 1   95

163 Color scheme 2   95

164 Color scheme 3   95

165 Four Square   96

166 Color scheme 1   96

167 Color scheme 2   96

168 Color scheme 3   96

169 Furrows   97

170 Color scheme 1   97

171 Color scheme 2   97

172 Color scheme 3   97

173 Waffle Stripes   98

174 Color scheme 1   98

175 Color scheme 2   98

176 Color scheme 3   98

177 Patch   99

178 Color scheme 1   99

179 Color scheme 2 99

180 Color scheme 3 99

181 Solid Leaf 100

182 Color scheme 1 100

183 Color scheme 2 100

184 Color scheme 3 100

185 Counterpoint 101

186 Color scheme 1 101

187 Color scheme 2 101

188 Color scheme 3 101

189 Oblique Stripe 102

190 Color scheme 1 102

191 Color scheme 2 102

192 Color scheme 3 102

193 Ridges 103

194 Color scheme 1 103

195 Color scheme 2 103

196 Color scheme 3 103

197 Harris 104

198 Color scheme 1 104

199 Color scheme 2 104

200 Color scheme 3 104

201 V-stripes 105

202 Color scheme 1 105

203 Color scheme 2 105

204 Color scheme 3 105

205 Big Cross 106

206 Color scheme 1 106

207 Color scheme 2 106

208 Color scheme 3 106

209 Little Waves 107

210 Color scheme 1 107

211 Color scheme 2 107

212 Color scheme 3 107

CHAPTER 3

Techniques 108

Yarn choices 110

Abbreviations 111

How to start 112

Working the basic stitches 113

Working stitch patterns 115

Working increases
    and decreases 116

Techniques for
    multicolored knitting 119

Decorative techniques 121

Blocking 122

Knitting an edging 123

Care of afghans 125

Yarn list 126

Index 128

Suppliers 128

Introduction

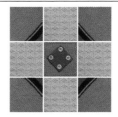

Knitting is one of the oldest ways of creating a fabric with yarn and the knitting of blocks that are subsequently joined together to make a larger piece of fabric has long been a favorite method of using up odds and ends of yarn. Because blocks are small, easily transportable units, you can work on them during a journey as well as while watching television or listening to music at home. The act of picking up yarn and needles and settling down to knit is the perfect way to unwind after a long, stressful day.

As well as instructions for making over 200 blocks, this book contains a selection of sample mix-and-match designs (see pages 12–27). These designs provide a useful jumping-off point and will encourage you to begin combining blocks according to your own design. The colors I've used are my own personal choice, and I can't stress strongly enough that you can work the blocks using any colors you like. I've included guidelines about using color (see page 14) and I hope these will help you to enjoy exploring the whole spectrum of colored yarns. My preference is for a pure wool yarn, as I find that this feels nicest in my hands and shows up the different stitches well. Please feel free to use whatever yarn suits you, whether it's made from wool, cotton, a synthetic fiber such as acrylic, or a wool/synthetic blend, but always keep to the same weight of yarn throughout a project.

How to use this book

MIX AND MATCH SECTION

The Mix and Match section, pages 12–27, takes you through the process of creating your own afghan design, giving you advice on combining blocks and exploring the world of color. There are also plans for making 11 afghans, blankets, and pillow covers using a selection of blocks from the book.

READING THE PLANS

Each design is accompanied by details of the finished size of the item, the type of yarn, colors, and needle size, as well as the names and reference numbers of the component blocks and how many to make of each one. This section also tells you how to finish off your blocks and join them together, and suggests a suitable edging to finish off your project.

SIZE

All the blocks are the same size, 6 in. (15cm) square, and have been worked using the same weight of yarn and size of needle, so any block can be mixed and matched with others at will.

QUANTITY AND COLORS

Each block used for the design is shown below the plan, accompanied by its pattern reference number, yarn colors, and how many of that block you need to make.

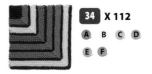

MIX AND MATCH SECTION

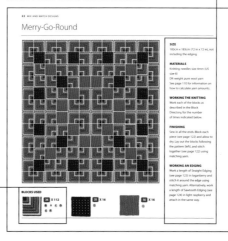

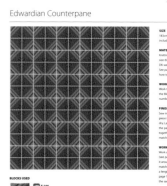

BLOCK DIRECTORY

The Block Directory contains a wide variety of block patterns, from well-loved traditional patterns to brand new designs. Each photographed block is accompanied by pattern instructions, yarn colors, and helpful symbols. The Directory is divided into two sections. Section one (pages 30–79) contains patterns for 100 blocks, while section two (pages 80–107) includes over 100 blocks, exploring alternative color combinations.

TECHNIQUES

The final section of this book contains detailed information on the abbreviations and how to work the stitches and techniques used. Different methods of joining blocks are demonstrated, as well as patterns for a selection of edgings to finish off your projects beautifully. Tips on choosing yarns are included, and at the end of the section is a list of the actual yarns used in this book.

UNDERSTANDING THE SYMBOLS

Each block pattern is accompanied by one or more symbols indicating how each pattern is worked, and a symbol indicating the pattern's degree of difficulty:

WORKED IN ROWS

This symbol shows that the block has been worked backward and forward in rows.

This symbol is used for blocks worked diagonally. You will find that some blocks, for example block 96 Button Up, are accompanied by both symbols as part of the pattern is worked in rows and part diagonally.

This symbol is used for blocks worked in L-shaped rows.

LEVEL OF DIFFICULTY

Beginner blocks

Some experience required

Challenging

BLOCK DIRECTORY: SECTION ONE

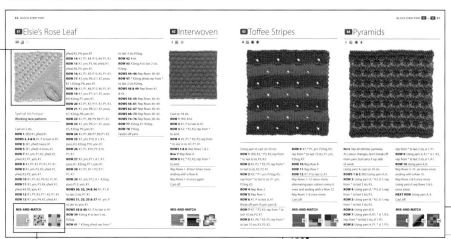

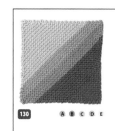

The second section of the book shows different color combinations for each block. Each yarn color is clearly referenced as used in the accompanying pattern.

BLOCK DIRECTORY: SECTION TWO

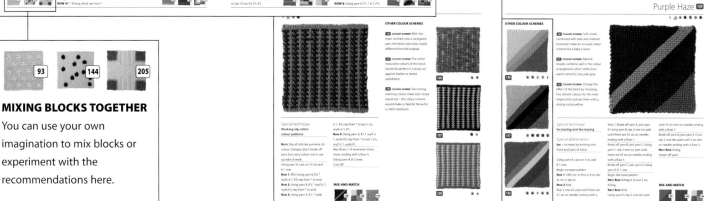

MIXING BLOCKS TOGETHER

You can use your own imagination to mix blocks or experiment with the recommendations here.

Mix and Match

This chapter shows you how to choose and combine blocks from the directory and includes a selection of colorful design ideas for making items in various sizes, from a large bed throw to a pillow cover, plus tips on how to plan your own design. A further section explores selecting and using your own choice of color.

Using color and texture

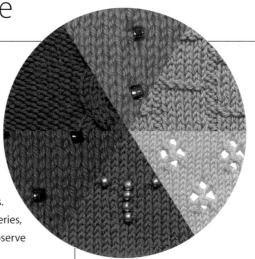

Color choice is a very personal thing—all colors combine and interact in different ways, which may appear more or less pleasing to the eye depending on the individual. The colors used to knit the blocks shown in the Block Directory are merely suggestions and reflect the author's own favorite color combinations, so please feel free to work the patterns in colors that you like. For color inspiration, look at flowers, plants, birds, animals, and insects. View paintings and other works of art in museums and galleries, look at how different colors have been put together, and observe the effects they create.

Color

It is useful to consider the basic guidelines on color theory at this stage, by investigating the standard "color wheel." This shows the three primary colors and other colors derived from them. The primary colors are red, yellow, and blue; these colors cannot be mixed from any other colors.

34

44

SECONDARY COLORS

The secondary colors are made by mixing two primary colors together: red and yellow make orange, yellow and blue make green, and red and blue make purple. These colors lie between each pair of primary colors on the color wheel.

36

132

COMPLEMENTARY COLORS

Colors that are opposite each other on the color wheel (for example blue and orange, red and green, yellow and purple) are complementary colors. At full strength, complementary colors may clash. If placed side by side, they can make each other appear more intense.

THE COLOR WHEEL

The color wheel is an arrangement of colors that demonstrates some basic aspects of color theory. This standard wheel displays the primary and secondary colors: red, orange, yellow, green, blue, and violet.

146

174

HARMONIOUS COLORS

Neighboring colors on the wheel, such as blue and purple, are harmonious. These tend to look good when used together as they each have a similar color makeup.

77

168

WARM COLORS

The red/orange/yellow half of the wheel consists of warm colors. It also includes other colors (for example, peachy pinks and lime greens) that contain some yellow.

COOL COLORS

14

84

Cool colors come from the opposite half of the wheel and include lavender, blue, green, turquoise, and blue-gray. There are warm and cool versions of every color, whether it is on the warm or cool side of the color wheel. Pink, for example, which is a warm color, also includes cool pinks such as clover and fuchsia, which contain quite a lot of blue. Blue is a cool color, but it includes warm blues such as ultramarine.

Making a palette

Make a personal yarn-color palette by cutting a strip of thin white card about 3 in. x 12 in. (8cm x 30cm). Punch holes along one long edge and loop lengths of your chosen yarns through the holes.

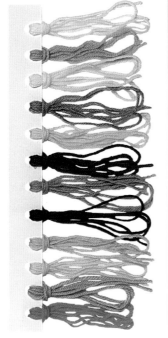

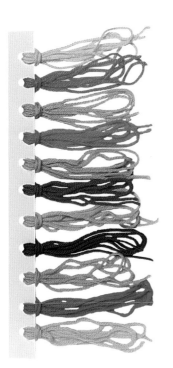

Color palettes: cool pastel and bright colors (left), neutrals and warm shades (above).

About texture

The surface of knit fabric can be smooth, lacy, or textured, depending on the stitch used. Smooth-surfaced blocks may be patterned by using different yarn colors to make stripes and other designs. Textured blocks have a raised surface made with knit and purl stitch patterns, bobbles, and cables. Lace blocks can be used alone or to add a touch of lightness to other block combinations.

SMOOTH BLOCKS

Smooth-surfaced blocks may be patterned with stripes, jacquard designs, and intarsia designs, and combined with both textured and lace blocks.

TEXTURED BLOCKS

Textured stitches add surface interest to large areas of solid color in a design, and also combine well with patterned blocks.

LACE BLOCKS

Lace stitches make perfect afghans for babies, as the knit fabric is soft and tends to drape well, whether used as a crib cover or a shawl for wrapping baby in.

Planning your designs

All 212 blocks in the Block Directory are the same size: 6 in. (15cm) square. You can put them together in thousands of combinations, according to your own design, to make items such as an afghan or throw, a blanket, or a pillow cover. The size of the finished item depends on its use—a blanket to cover a double bed will need to be much larger than an everyday throw that you snuggle into when reading or watching television. As a rough guide, a throw that will be draped over a couch or chair should be about 48 in. (122cm) square.

Planning a design

It's a good idea to start by making a full-color visual plan, then you can be sure you'll be happy with the appearance and size of the finished item. First, mark out the outline of the required number of blocks on graph paper, making a grid of squares.

MAKING A PAPER PLAN

Make each block about 1 in. (2.5cm) square. Roughly color the squares with pencils or felt-tip markers in the colors and patterns of the blocks you have chosen.

At the side of the plan, write down the number of blocks you need to make and details of the yarn colors you have selected. There's information on page 110 telling you how to calculate the amount of yarn you will need to buy.

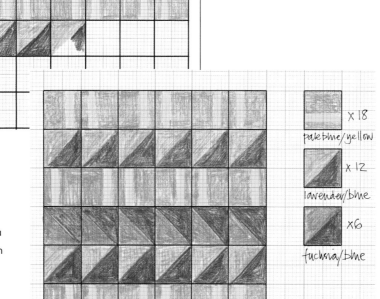

x 18
pale blue/yellow

x 12
lavender/blue

x 6
fuchsia/blue

Creating patterns

Many of the blocks can be combined in more than one way. When you arrange identical blocks into groups of four or more, and start turning some of the blocks in other directions, different patterns start to appear. For example, take a block made from two identical triangles (block 69, Twin Triangles) and see how many combinations you can make using four or more blocks.

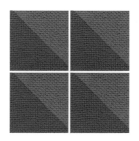

Twin Triangles, block 69

SAWTOOTH

Four blocks, placed as shown, make a sawtooth pattern that could be repeated across a whole afghan using colors that gradually shade into each other—think shades of green from dark to light, then changing through yellow and amber into shades of orange and rust.

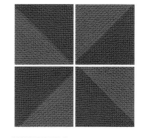

WINDMILL

Make a classic windmill pattern by starting with the top right block the correct way up, then turning the other blocks 90° away from each other in turn.

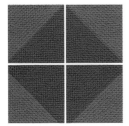

DIAMOND

Create a simple diamond shape by combining the four blocks so that one color meets in the centre. Start with the top left block the correct way up, then turn the other blocks 90º away from each other in turn.

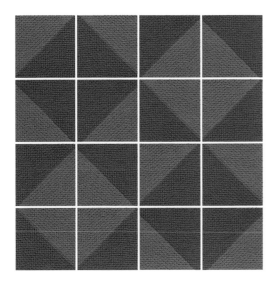

REPEATING DIAMONDS

Make a second diamond by turning individual blocks so that the diamond is now made from the background color. Add two more four-block diamonds below the first two to make a repeating pattern.

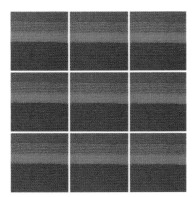

Soft Stripes, block 164

STRIPES

Striped blocks offer a range of design possibilities. Using a simple striped block (block 164, Soft Stripes, color scheme 3), make vertical or horizontal stripes by arranging several blocks with the top edges facing the same way.

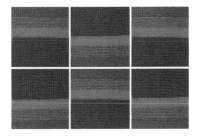

BROKEN STRIPES

Broken-stripe patterns are made by alternating the top and bottom of each block. Create a different effect by turning some blocks vertically.

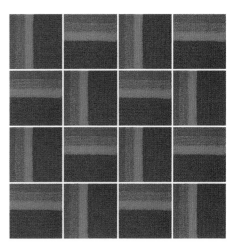

STEPPED ZIGZAG

Make this pattern by turning alternate blocks vertically and horizontally. The pattern will vary depending on the width and complexity of the stripes on the actual block you use.

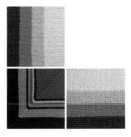

FRAMING A PATTERN

To make a "frame" around your afghan, combine striped blocks and corner blocks in matching or coordinating colors. Here striped blocks (block 162, Soft Stripes, color scheme 1) have been arranged around the edge of a design together with corner blocks (block 101, Blue Seas).

Heart's Delight

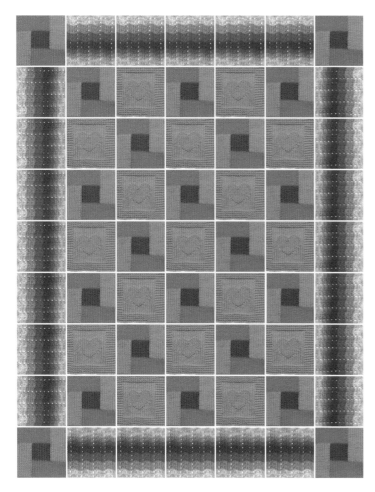

SIZE

42 in. x 54 in. (107cm x 137cm), not including the edging

MATERIALS

Knitting needles size 6 (4mm)

DK-weight pure wool yarn

See page 110 for information on how to calculate yarn amounts.

WORKING THE KNITTING

Work each of the blocks as described in the Block Directory, for the number of times indicated below.

FINISHING

Sew in all the ends. Block each piece (see page 122) and allow to dry. Lay out the blocks following the pattern (left), and stitch together (see page 122) using matching yarn.

WORKING AN EDGING

Work a length of Sawtooth Edging (see page 124) in clover pink and stitch it around the edge using matching yarn. Alternatively, work a length of Straight Edging (see page 123) in magenta and attach in the same way.

BLOCKS USED

  17 X 17

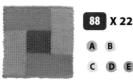 **88** X 22

A B

C D E

 210 X 24

 A B C D

Bobble Fantasy

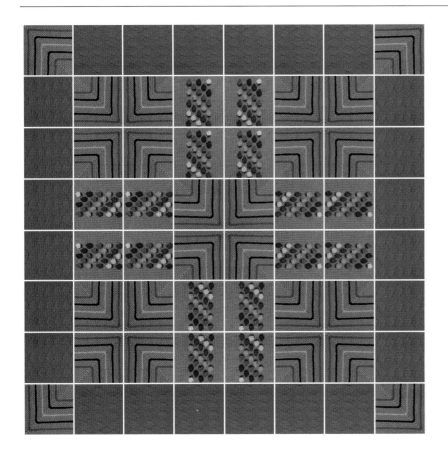

SIZE
48 in. x 48 in. (122cm x 122cm), not including the edging

MATERIALS
Knitting needles size 6 (4mm)
DK-weight pure wool yarn
See page 110 for information on how to calculate
yarn amounts.

WORKING THE KNITTING
Work each of the blocks as described in the Block Directory,
for the number of times indicated below.

FINISHING
Sew in all the ends. Block each piece (see page 122) and
allow to dry. Lay out the blocks following the pattern (left),
and stitch together (see page 122) using matching yarn.

WORKING AN EDGING
Work a length of Straight Edging (see page 123) in larkspur
and stitch it around the edge using matching yarn.
Alternatively, work a length of Ruffled Edging (see page
125) in larkspur and attach in the same way.

BLOCKS USED

  44 X 16
Ⓐ Ⓑ C
Ⓓ Ⓔ Ⓕ

 90 X 24
Ⓑ

  146 X 24
Ⓐ Ⓑ Ⓒ Ⓓ

Blue Geometric

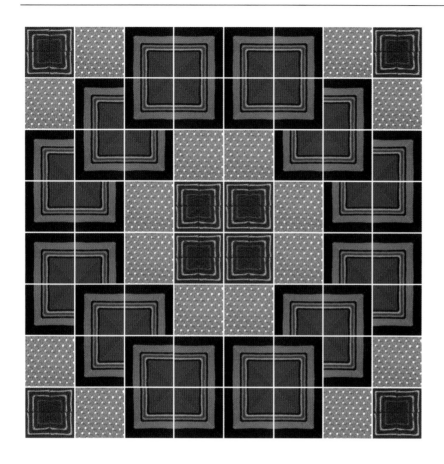

SIZE
48 in. x 48 in. (122cm x 122cm), not including the edging

MATERIALS
Knitting needles size 6 (4mm)
DK-weight pure wool yarn
See page 110 for information on how to calculate
yarn amounts.

WORKING THE KNITTING
Work each of the blocks as described in the Block Directory,
for the number of times indicated below.

FINISHING
Sew in all the ends. Block each piece (see page 122) and
allow to dry. Lay out the blocks following the pattern (left),
and stitch together (see page 122) using matching yarn.

WORKING AN EDGING
Work a length of Straight Edging (see page 123) in mariner
blue and stitch it around the edge using matching yarn.
Alternatively, work a length of Zigzag Edging (see page
123) in bluebell and attach in the same way.

BLOCKS USED

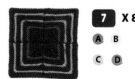 **7** X 8
Ⓐ Ⓑ
Ⓒ Ⓓ

 74 X 16
ⓒ

 101 X 40
Ⓐ Ⓑ Ⓒ Ⓓ

Modern Times

SIZE
36 in. x 48 in. (91cm x 122cm), not including the edging

MATERIALS
Knitting needles size 6 (4mm)
DK-weight pure wool yarn
See page 110 for information on how to calculate
yarn amounts.

WORKING THE KNITTING
Work each of the blocks as described in the Block Directory,
for the number of times indicated below.

FINISHING
Sew in all the ends. Block each piece (see page 122) and allow
to dry. Lay out the blocks following the pattern (left), and
stitch together (see page 122) using matching yarn.

WORKING AN EDGING
Work a length of Curly Fringe (see page 125) in sunshine
yellow and stitch it around the edge using matching yarn.
Alternatively, work a length of Ruffled Edging (see page 125)
in orange and attach in the same way.

BLOCKS USED

  46 X 24
Ⓐ Ⓑ

  47 X 12
Ⓐ Ⓑ Ⓒ

  168 X 12
Ⓐ Ⓑ Ⓒ Ⓓ

Merry-Go-Round

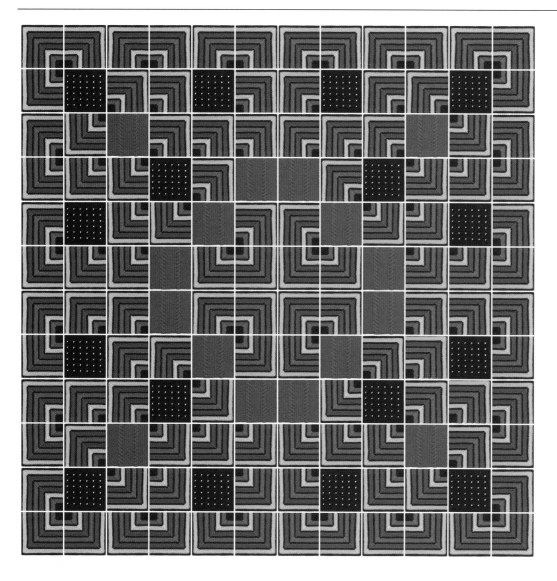

SIZE
72 in. x 72 in. (183cm x 183cm), not including the edging

MATERIALS
Knitting needles size 6 (4mm)
DK-weight pure wool yarn
See page 110 for information on how to calculate yarn amounts.

WORKING THE KNITTING
Work each of the blocks as described in the Block Directory, for the number of times indicated below.

FINISHING
Sew in all the ends. Block each piece (see page 122) and allow to dry. Lay out the blocks following the pattern (left), and stitch together (see page 122) using matching yarn.

WORKING AN EDGING
Work a length of Straight Edging (see page 123) in loganberry and stitch it around the edge using matching yarn. Alternatively, work a length of Sawtooth Edging (see page 124) in light raspberry and attach in the same way.

BLOCKS USED

 **34** X 112
A B C D
E F

 **35** X 16

 **16** X 16

Edwardian Counterpane

SIZE
72 in. x 72 in. (183cm x 183cm), not including the edging

MATERIALS
Knitting needles size 6 (4mm)
DK-weight pure wool yarn
See page 110 for information on how to calculate yarn amounts.

WORKING THE KNITTING
Work the blocks as described in the Block Directory, for the number of times indicated below.

FINISHING
Sew in all the ends. Block each piece (see page 122) and allow to dry. Lay out the blocks following the pattern (left), and stitch together (see page 122) using matching yarn.

WORKING AN EDGING
Work a length of Leaf Edging (see page 124) in sage and stitch it around the edge using matching yarn. Alternatively, work a length of Straight Edging (see page 123) in rust and attach in the same way.

BLOCKS USED

 149 **X 144**

Ⓐ Ⓑ Ⓒ Ⓓ

Bright and Bold

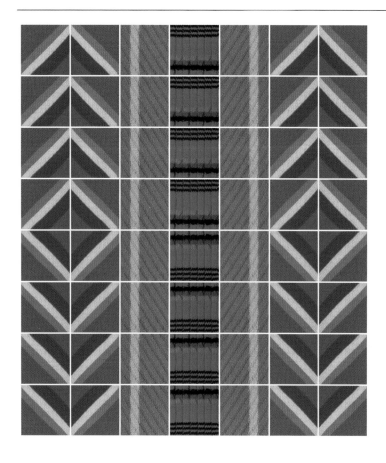

SIZE
42 in. x 48 in. (107cm x 122cm), not including the edging

MATERIALS
Knitting needles size 6 (4mm)
DK-weight pure wool yarn
See page 110 for information on how to calculate yarn amounts.

WORKING THE KNITTING
Work each of the blocks as described in the Block Directory, for the number of times indicated below.

FINISHING
Sew in all the ends. Block each piece (see page 122) and allow to dry. Lay out the blocks following the pattern (left), and stitch together (see page 122) using matching yarn.

WORKING AN EDGING
Work a length of Ruffled Edging (see page 125) in fuchsia and stitch it around the edge using matching yarn. Alternatively, work a length of Straight Edging (see page 123) in elderberry and attach in the same way.

BLOCKS USED

 87 X 16

 120 X 8

 132 X 32

Nocturne

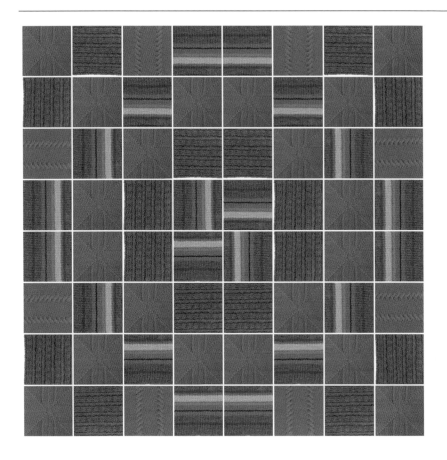

SIZE
48 in. x 48 in. (122cm x 122cm), not including the edging

MATERIALS
Knitting needles size 6 (4mm)
DK-weight pure wool yarn
See page 110 for information on how to calculate yarn amounts.

WORKING THE KNITTING
Work each of the blocks as described in the Block Directory, for the number of times indicated below.

FINISHING
Sew in all the ends. Block each piece (see page 122) and allow to dry. Lay out the blocks following the pattern (left), and stitch together (see page 122) using matching yarn.

WORKING AN EDGING
Work a length of Zigzag Edging (see page 123) in granite and stitch it around the edge using matching yarn. Alternatively, work a length of Sawtooth Edging (see page 124) in lavender and attach in the same way.

BLOCKS USED

 16 X 8

 49 X 16

 76 X 20
A B C D
E F

 208 X 20
A B

Buttoned Pillow

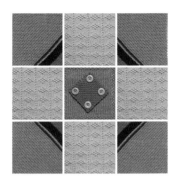

BLOCKS USED

31 X 8

○

45 X 8

Ⓐ Ⓑ Ⓒ Ⓓ Ⓔ

96 X 2

Ⓐ Ⓑ

SIZE

To fit pillow form 18 in. x 18 in. (45cm x 45cm)

MATERIALS

Knitting needles size 6 (4mm)
DK-weight pure wool yarn
See page 110 for information on how to calculate yarn amounts.

WORKING THE KNITTING

Work each of the blocks as described in the Block Directory, for the number of times indicated at left.

FINISHING

Sew in all the ends. Block each piece (see page 122) and allow to dry. Lay out the blocks following the pattern (above) to make two identical pieces for the front and back of the pillow. Stitch the blocks together (see page 122) using matching yarn. Place the front and back pieces together, with right sides facing, and stitch three of the sides. Turn right side out, insert the pillow form, and stitch the edges of the opening together.

Holiday Pillow

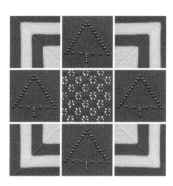

BLOCKS USED

57 X 8

Ⓐ Ⓑ Ⓒ

58 X 2

●

59 X 8

● ○ x 31

SIZE

To fit pillow form 18 in. x 18 in. (45cm x 45cm)

MATERIALS

Knitting needles size 6 (4mm)
DK-weight pure wool yarn
See page 110 for information on how to calculate yarn amounts

WORKING THE KNITTING

Work each of the blocks as described in the Block Directory, for the number of times indicated at left.

FINISHING

Sew in all the ends. Block each piece (see page 122) and allow to dry. Lay out the blocks following the pattern (above) to make two identical pieces for the front and back of the pillow. Stitch the blocks together (see page 122) using matching yarn. Place the front and back pieces together, with right sides facing, and stitch three of the sides. Turn right side out, insert the pillow form, and stitch the edges of the opening together.

Baby Lace

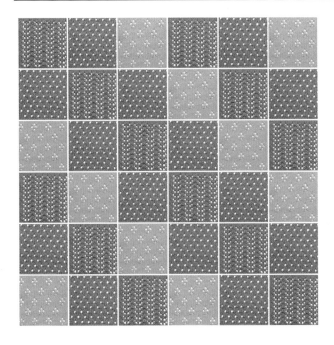

SIZE

36 in. x 36 in. (91cm x 91cm), not including the edging

MATERIALS

Knitting needles size 6 (4mm)

DK-weight pure wool yarn

See page 110 for information on how to calculate yarn amounts

WORKING THE KNITTING

Work each of the blocks as described in the Block Directory, for the number of times indicated below.

FINISHING

Sew in all the ends. Block each piece (see page 122) and allow to dry. Lay out the blocks following the pattern (left), and stitch together (see page 122) using matching yarn.

WORKING AN EDGING

Work a length of Zigzag Edging (see page 123) in pale turquoise and stitch it around the edge using matching yarn. Alternatively, work a length of Ruffled Edging (see page 125) in sky blue and attach in the same way.

BLOCKS USED

  6 X 12

 74 X 14

 93 X 10

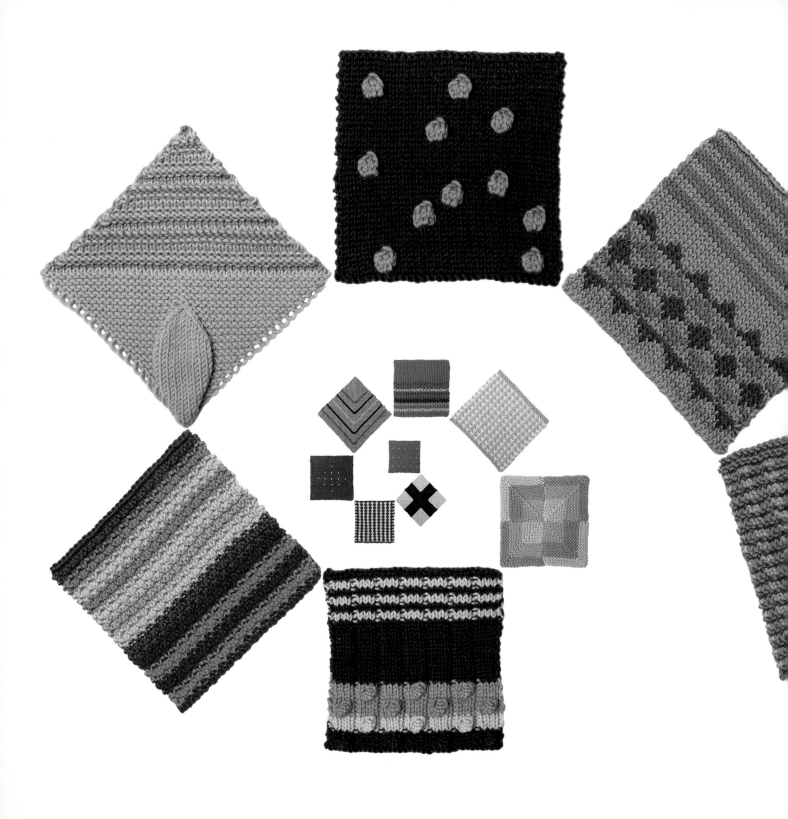

Block Directory

The Block Directory contains photographs and patterns for over 200 knitted blocks. Each block is graded by degree of difficulty so you can choose the ones which suit your own skill level. In the last section, each main pattern is shown in its original colors, along with three different color schemes to illustrate the variety of effects you can achieve.

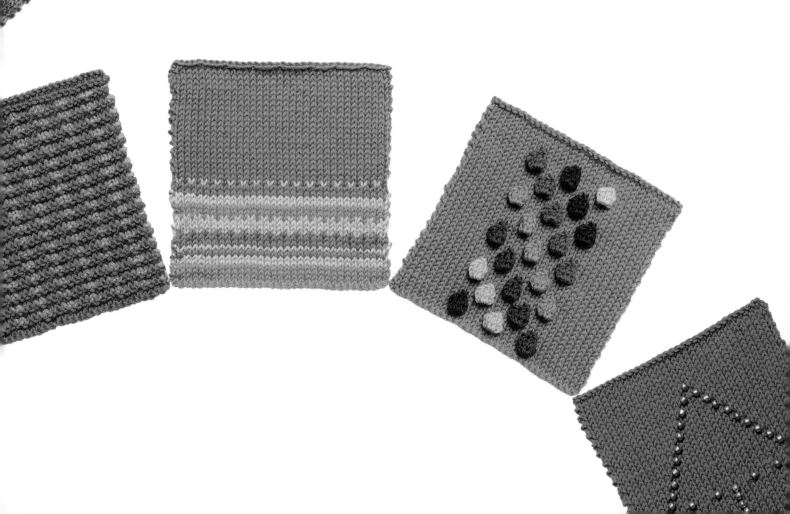

① Speckle

Special technique
Working Fair Isle patterns

YARN A   YARN B   YARN C

Using yarn A, CO 35 sts and P one row (WS).

Starting at the bottom right-hand corner of the chart, work the 37-row pattern, reading odd-numbered rows (right side rows—K all sts) from right to left and even-numbered rows (wrong side rows—P all sts) from left to right. Using yarn A, K 1 row, P 1 row. BO.

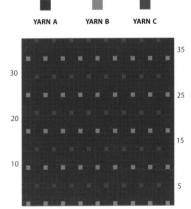

MIX-AND-MATCH

 2

 4

 190

② Offset

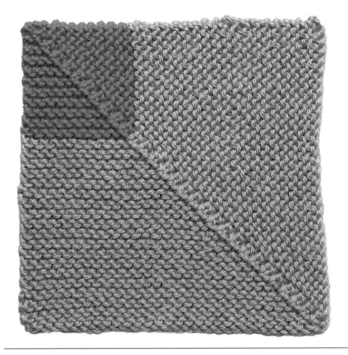

Special technique
Double decreasing

Using yarn A, CO 61 sts and K 1 row.

ROW 1: (RS) K29, sl 1, K2tog, psso, K29.

ROW 2: Knit.

ROW 3: K28, sl 1, K2tog, psso, K28.

ROW 4: Knit.

Cont working in this way, dec 2 sts at center of every RS (odd-numbered) row until 25 sts rem on needle, ending with a WS row. Break off yarn A, join yarn B and

cont in patt until 3 sts rem on needle, ending with a WS row.

NEXT ROW: K3tog.

Fasten off yarn.

MIX-AND-MATCH

 48

 94

 196

3 Double Eyelets

4 Threaded Ribbons

ROWS 15 & 16: Rep Rows 1 & 2.

ROWS 17–20: Using yarn D, rep Rows 7–10.

ROWS 21–28: Rep Rows 1–4 twice more, ending with a Row 4.

ROWS 29 & 30: Rep Rows 1 & 2.

ROWS 31–34: Rep Rows 17–20.

ROWS 35–38: Rep Rows 1–4.

ROWS 39 & 40: Rep Rows 1 & 2.

ROWS 41–44: Rep Rows 7–10.

ROWS 45–48: Rep Rows 1–4.

ROWS 49 & 50: Rep Rows 1 & 2.

BO.

Special technique
Working lace patterns

CO 33 sts.

ROW 1: (RS) Knit.

ROW 2 AND EVERY ALT ROW: K1, P to last st, K1.

ROW 3: K4, * K2tog, YO, K1, YO, sl 1, K1, psso, K5; rep from * to last 9 sts, K2tog, YO, K1, YO, sl 1, K1, psso, K4.

ROW 5: Knit.

ROW 7: K2, * YO, sl 1 , K1, psso, K5, K2tog, YO, K1; rep from * to last st, K1.

ROW 8: K1, P to last st, K1.

Rep Rows 1–8 four times more, ending with a Row 8.
Rep Row 1 once more.
BO.

MIX-AND-MATCH

Special technique
Working slip-stitch color patterns

NOTE Slip all stitches purlwise, keeping yarn on wrong side of work. At color changes, don't break off main yarn, but carry it up side of work.

Using yarn A, CO 35 sts.

ROW 1: (RS) Using yarn A, K.

ROW 2: Using yarn A, K1, P to last st, K1.

ROW 3: Using yarn B, K1, * sl 1, K3; rep from * to last 2 sts, sl 1, K1.

ROW 4: Using yarn B, P1, * sl 1, P3; rep from * to last 2 sts, sl 1, P1.

ROWS 5 & 6: Rep Rows 1 & 2.

ROW 7: Using yarn C, K3, * sl 1, K3; rep from * to end.

ROW 8: Using yarn C, P3, * sl 1, P3; rep from * to end.

ROWS 9 & 10: Rep Rows 7 & 8.

ROWS 11–14: Rep Rows 1–4.

MIX-AND-MATCH

5 Mini Stripes

NOTE At color changes, don't break off yarn, but carry color not in use up side of work.

Using yarn A, CO 33 sts.

ROW 1: (RS) Using yarn A, K.

ROW 2: Using yarn A, K1, P to last st, K1.

ROW 3: Using yarn B, K.

ROW 4: Using yarn B, K1, P to last st, K1.

Rep Rows 1–4 nine times more, ending with a Row 4.

Rep Rows 1 & 2 once more.

BO.

MIX-AND-MATCH

6 Lace Chevrons

Special technique

Working lace patterns

CO 34 sts and K 2 rows.

ROW 1: (RS) Knit.

ROW 2: K1, P to last st, K1.

ROWS 3 & 4: Rep Rows 1 & 2.

ROW 5: K4, * K2tog, YO, K1, YO, sl 1, K1, psso, K2; rep from * to last 2 sts, K2.

ROW 6: K1, P to last st, K1.

ROW 7: K3, * K2tog, YO, K3, YO, sl 1, K1, psso; rep from * to last 3 sts, K3.

ROW 8: K1, P to last st, K1.

Rep Rows 5–8 nine times more, ending with a Row 8.

Rep Rows 1–3 once more.

BO.

MIX-AND-MATCH

7 Target

Special technique
Double decreasing

NOTE When introducing a stripe color, don't break off the main yarn. Instead, work the two-row stripe in the required color, break off the contrast yarn and continue knitting with the main yarn.

Using yarn A, CO 31 sts and K 1 row.

ROW 1: (RS) K14, sl 1, K2tog, psso, K14.

ROW 2: Knit.

ROW 3: K13, sl 1, K2tog, psso, K13.

ROW 4: Knit.

Cont working in this way using yarn A, dec 2 sts at the center of every RS (odd-numbered) row and working rows in contrast yarn following this color sequence:

ROWS 5 & 6: Yarn B.

ROWS 11 & 12: Yarn C.

ROWS 17 & 18: Yarn D.

Cont in yarn A only until 3 sts rem on the needle, ending with a WS row.

NEXT ROW: K3tog.

Fasten off yarn.

Make three more identical blocks. Using the photograph as a guide to position, join the four blocks together using the overcast method of joining shown on page 122.

MIX-AND-MATCH

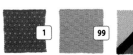

8 Little Blocks

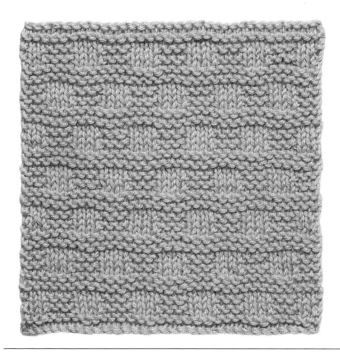

CO 33 sts.

ROW 1 AND EVERY ALT ROW: (RS) Knit.

ROW 2: Knit.

ROWS 4 & 6: P3, * K3, P3; rep from * to end.

ROWS 8 & 10: Knit.

ROWS 12 & 14: K3, * P3, K3; rep from * to end.

ROW 16: Knit.

Rep Rows 1–16 twice more, ending with a Row 16.

Rep Rows 1–9 once more.

BO.

MIX-AND-MATCH

9 Pinstripes

10 Horizontal Ridges

Special technique
**Working slip-stitch
color patterns**

NOTE Slip all stitches purlwise,
keeping yarn on wrong side of
work. At color changes, don't
break off yarn, but carry color not
in use up side of work.
Using yarn A, CO 39 sts.
ROW 1: (RS) Using yarn B, K2, * sl
1, K1; rep from * to last st, K1.
ROW 2: Using yarn B, K1, P1, * sl 1,
P1; rep from * to last st, K1.
ROW 3: Using yarn A, * K1, sl 1; rep
from * to last st, K1.

ROW 4: Using yarn A, K1, * sl 1, P1;
rep from * to last 2 sts, sl 1, K1.
Rep Rows 1–4 seventeen times
more, ending with a Row 4.
BO.

CO 33 sts.
ROW 1: (RS) Knit.
ROW 2: K1, P to last st, K1.
ROWS 3 & 4: Knit.
ROW 5: K1, P to last st, K1.
ROW 6: K1, P to last st, K1.
Rep Rows 1–6 six times more,
ending with a Row 6.
Rep Rows 1 & 2 once more.
BO.

MIX-AND-MATCH

 175 179 206

MIX-AND-MATCH

 71 87 132

11 Ritzy

Special techniques
Working color patterns by the intarsia method, applying beads with slip stitch

| BEAD | YARN A | YARN B | YARN C |

NOTE Before casting on, thread 18 beads onto yarn A. Apply each bead with a slip stitch—bring yarn to front of work, slip next stitch, slide bead down yarn, take yarn to back of work. Slip all stitches purlwise.

Using yarn A, CO 33 sts. Starting at the bottom right-hand corner of the chart, work the 42-row pattern, reading odd-numbered rows (right side rows —K all sts) from right to left and even-numbered rows (wrong side rows—P all sts) from left to right and applying beads at the positions indicated. BO.

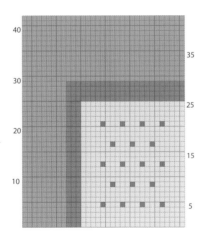

MIX-AND-MATCH

48 77 79

12 Surface Cables

Special technique
Working cables

Special abbreviations
C4B = slip next 2 sts onto cable needle, hold at back of work, knit next 2 sts from left-hand needle, knit stitches from cable needle.
C4F = slip next 2 sts onto cable needle, hold at front of work, knit next 2 sts from left-hand needle, knit stitches from cable needle.

CO 44 sts.
ROW 1: (RS) P2, * K4, P2; rep from * to end.

ROW 2 AND EVERY ALT ROW: K2, * P4, K2; rep from * to end.
ROW 3: P2, * C4B, P2; rep from * to end.
ROW 5: Rep Row 1.
ROW 7: P2, * C4F, P2; rep from * to end.
ROW 8: K2, * P4, K2; rep from * to end.
Rep Rows 1–8 five times more, ending with a Row 8. BO.

MIX-AND-MATCH

45 130 148

13 Ribby

CO 34 sts.

ROW 1: (RS) K1, P2, K1tbl, P2,
* K4, P2, K1tbl, P2; rep from * to
last st, K1.

ROW 2: K3, P1tbl, K2, * P4, K2,
P1tbl, K2; rep from * to last st, K1.
Rep Rows 1 & 2 twenty-one times
more, ending with a Row 2.
BO.

MIX-AND-MATCH

14 Troika

Special technique
Working Fair Isle patterns

Using yarn A, CO 37 sts. Starting at
the bottom right-hand corner of
the chart, work the 40-row
pattern, reading odd-numbered
rows (right side rows—K all sts)
from right to left and even-
numbered rows (wrong side rows
—P all sts) from left to right. BO.

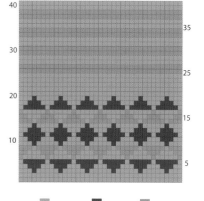

YARN A   YARN B   YARN C

MIX-AND-MATCH

15 Twilight

Special technique
Working slip-stitch color patterns

NOTE Slip all stitches purlwise. At color changes, don't break off main yarn, but carry it up side of work.

Using yarn A, CO 35 sts.

ROW 1: (WS) Using yarn A, K1, sl 1, * P3, sl 1 with yarn at back; rep from * to last 5 sts, P3, sl 1 with yarn at back, K1.

ROW 2: Using yarn A, K1, sl 1 with yarn at back, * K3, sl 1 with yarn at back; rep from * to last st, K1.

ROW 3: Using yarn B, K1, P2, * sl 1 with yarn at back, P3; rep from * to last 4 sts, sl 1 with yarn at back, P2, K1.

ROW 4: Using yarn B, K3, * sl 1 with yarn at back, K3; rep from * to end.

Rep Rows 1–4 six times more, ending with a Row 4.

Break off yarns A and B; join yarns C and D.

Cont in patt using yarn C instead of yarn A, and yarn D instead of yarn B.

Rep Rows 1–4 four times more, ending with a Row 4.

Break off yarns C and D; join yarns E and F.

Cont in patt using yarn E instead of yarn A, and yarn F instead of yarn B.

Rep Rows 1–4 three times more, ending with a Row 4.

Using yarn E, rep Row 1 once more.

BO.

MIX-AND-MATCH

16 Mirror Image

Special technique
Working cables

Special abbreviations
C6B = slip next 3 sts onto cable needle, hold at back of work, knit next 3 sts from left-hand needle, then knit stitches from cable needle.

C6F = slip next 3 sts onto cable needle, hold at front of work, knit next 3 sts from left-hand needle, then knit stitches from cable needle.

CO 38 sts.

ROW 1: (RS) K1, * P8, K6; rep from * to last 9 sts, P8, K1.

ROW 2: K9, P6, K8, P6, K9.

ROW 3: K1, P8, C6B, P8, C6F, P8, K1.

ROW 4: K9, P6, K8, P6, K9.

Rep Rows 1–4 eleven times more, ending with a Row 4.

BO.

MIX-AND-MATCH

17 Reversed Heart

Special technique
Working knit and purl patterns from a chart

CO 33 sts.
Starting at the bottom right-hand corner of the chart, work the 45-row pattern, reading odd-numbered rows (right side rows) from right to left and even-numbered rows (wrong side rows) from left to right.
BO.

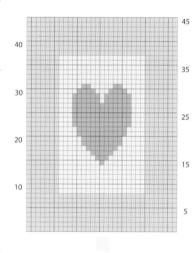

K on RS rows, P on WS rows

K on both RS and WS rows

P on RS rows, K on WS rows

MIX-AND-MATCH

 128   155   210

18 Flowing Pinks

ROW 8: Using yarn A, K1, P4, * sl 1, P5; rep from * to last 6 sts, sl 1, P4, K1.
Rep Rows 1–8 five times more, ending with a Row 8.
BO.

Special technique
Working slip-stitch color patterns

NOTE Slip all stitches purlwise, keeping yarn on wrong side of work. At color changes, don't break off yarn, but carry color not in use up side of work.
Using yarn A, CO 35 sts.
ROW 1: (RS) Using yarn A, K.
ROW 2: Using yarn A, K1, P to last st, K1.
ROW 3: Using yarn B, K1, * sl 3, K3; rep from * to last 4 sts, sl 3, K1.
ROW 4: Using yarn B, K1, P1, * sl 1, P5; rep from * to last 3 sts, sl 1, P1, K1.
ROW 5: Using yarn B, K.
ROW 6: Using yarn B, K1, P to last st, K1.
ROW 7: Using yarn A, K4, * sl 3, K3; rep from * to last st, K1.

MIX-AND-MATCH

 88   155   165

19 Little Knots

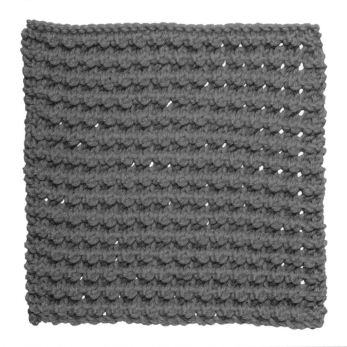

20 Shady Ladders

Special abbreviation

PU = pick up strand between this and next stitch, and knit it.

NOTE Count stitches only on Rows 3 and 4. Block well, as this stitch pattern pulls on the bias.
CO 33 sts.
ROW 1: (RS) K1, * K2tog; rep from * to last 2 sts, K2.
ROW 2: K1, * K1, pu; rep from * to last 2 sts, K2.
ROW 3: Knit.
ROW 4: K1, P to last st, K1.
Rep Rows 1–4 thirteen times more, ending with a Row 4.
Rep Rows 1–3 once more.
BO.

MIX-AND-MATCH

 17 36 193

Special technique

Working slip-stitch color patterns

NOTE Slip all stitches purlwise, keeping yarn on wrong side of work. At color changes, don't break off yarn, but carry color not in use up side of work.
Using yarn A, CO 35 sts.
ROW 1: (RS) Using yarn A, K2, * sl 1, K5; rep from * to last 3 sts, sl 1, K2.
ROW 2: Using yarn A, K1, P1, sl 1, * P5, sl 1; rep from * to last 2 sts, P1, K1.
ROW 3: Using yarn B, * K5, sl 1; rep from * to last 5 sts, K5.
ROW 4: Using yarn B, * K5, sl 1; rep from * to last 5 sts, K5.
Rep Rows 1–4 twice more, ending with a Row 4.
Break off yarn A; join yarn C.

Rep Rows 1–4 three times more, replacing yarn A with yarn C, and ending with a Row 4.
Break off yarn C; join yarn D.
Rep Rows 1–4 three times more, replacing yarn A with yarn D, and ending with a Row 4.
Break off yarn D, join yarn E.
Rep Rows 1–4 three times more, replacing yarn A with yarn E, and ending with a Row 4.
Break off yarn E, join yarn F.
Rep Rows 1–4 three times more, replacing yarn A with yarn F, and ending with a Row 4.
NEXT ROW: Using yarn F, K.
BO.

MIX-AND-MATCH

 104 109 175

21 Tabard

Using yarn A, CO 34 sts.
Break off yarn A; join yarn B.
ROW 1: (RS) * K1, P1; rep from *
to end.
ROW 2: K1, P to last st, K1.
ROW 3: * P1, K1; rep from * to end.
ROW 4: K1, P to last st, K1.
Rep Rows 1–4 eleven times
more, ending with a Row 4 and
changing yarns in the following
sequence:
4 rows in yarn A, 4 rows in yarn B,
4 rows in yarn A, 4 rows in yarn C,
4 rows in yarn D, 4 rows in yarn E,
4 rows in yarn D, 4 rows in yarn F,
4 rows in yarn D, 4 rows in yarn F,

4 rows in yarn C.
BO.

MIX-AND-MATCH

 23
 49
 82

22 Plain Leaf

Special abbreviation

M1 = make an extra stitch at
beginning of row by working
yarn over before knitting first
stitch on needle.

Using yarn A, CO 3 sts.
ROW 1: M1, K3.
ROW 2: M1, K4.
ROW 3: M1, K2, YO, K1, YO, K2.
ROW 4: M1, K2, P3, K3.
ROW 5: M1, K4, YO, K1, YO, K4.
ROW 6: M1, K3, P5, K4.
ROW 7: M1, K6, YO, K1, YO, K6.
ROW 8: M1, K4, P7, K5.
ROW 9: M1, K8, YO, K1, YO, K8.
ROW 10: M1, K5, P9, K6.
ROW 11: M1, K10, YO, K1, YO, K10.
ROW 12: M1, K6, P11, K7.
ROW 13: M1, K12, YO, K1, YO, K12.
ROW 14: M1, K7, P13, K8.
ROW 15: M1, K14, YO, K1, YO, K14.
ROW 16: M1, K8, P15, K9.

ROW 17: M1, K9, sl 1, K1, psso, K11,
K2tog, K9.
ROW 18: M1, K9, P13, K10.
ROW 19: M1, K10, sl 1, K1, psso, K9,
K2tog, K10.
ROW 20: M1, K10, P11, K11.
ROW 21: M1, K11, sl 1, K1, psso, K7,
K2tog, K11.
ROW 22: M1, K11, P9, K12.
ROW 23: M1, K12, sl 1, K1, psso, K5,
K2tog, K12.
ROW 24: M1, K12, P7, K13.
ROW 25: M1, K13, sl 1, K1, psso, K3,
K2tog, K13.
ROW 26: M1, K13, P5, K14.
ROW 27: M1, K14, sl 1, K1, psso, K1,
K2tog, K14.
ROW 28: M1, K14, P3, K15.
ROW 29: M1, K15, K3tog, K15.
ROWS 30–38: M1, K to end
(41 sts).
ROW 39: K2 tog, K39.
ROW 40: K2 tog, K38.
Cont dec 1 st in this way until 4
sts rem on needle.
NEXT ROW: K2tog twice.
BO.

MIX-AND-MATCH

 103
 107
 192

23 Zigzag Eyelets

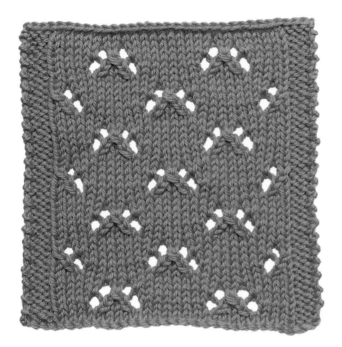

24 Ridged Blocks

A B

Special technique
Working lace patterns

CO 33 sts.

ROW 1: (RS) K1, P3, K to last 4 sts, P3, K1.

ROW 2 AND EVERY ALT ROW: K4, P to last 4 sts, K4.

ROW 3: K1, P3, K4, YO, sl 1, K1, psso, K1, K2tog, YO, K7, YO, sl 1, K1, psso, K1, K2tog, YO, K4, P3, K1.

ROW 5: K1, P3, K5, YO, sl 1, K2tog, psso, YO, K9, YO, sl 1, K2tog, psso, YO, K5, P3, K1.

ROW 7: K1, P3, K to last 4 sts, P3, K1.

ROW 9: K1, P3, K1, * K2tog, YO, K7, YO, sl 1, K1, psso, K1; rep from * to last 4 sts, P3, K1.

ROW 11: K1, P3, K2tog, YO, K9, YO, sl 1, K2tog, psso, YO, K9, YO, sl 1, K1, psso, P3, K1.

ROW 12: K4, P to last 4 sts, K4.

Rep Rows 1–12 twice more, ending with a Row 12.

Rep Rows 1–8 once again. BO.

MIX-AND-MATCH

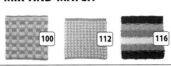

Special technique
Working slip-stitch color patterns

NOTE Slip all stitches purlwise, keeping yarn on wrong side of work. At color changes, don't break off yarn, but carry color not in use up side of work.

Using yarn A, CO 36 sts.

ROW 1: (RS) Using yarn A, K.

ROW 2: Using yarn A, K.

ROW 3: Using yarn B, K1, * sl 2, K2; rep from * to last 3 sts, sl 2, K1.

ROW 4: Using yarn B, K1, * sl 2, P2; rep from * to last 3 sts, sl 2, K1.

Rep Rows 1–4 fifteen times more, ending with a Row 4.

Rep Rows 1 & 2 once more.

NEXT ROW: Using yarn A, K. BO.

MIX-AND-MATCH

25 Wavy Ribbons

CO 34 sts.

ROW 1: (RS) K1, P1, K6, * P2, K6; rep from * to last 2 sts, P1, K1.

ROW 2: * K2, P6; rep from * to last 2 sts, K2.

ROW 3: K1, P1, K6, * P2, K6; rep to last 2 sts, P1, K1.

ROW 4: K2, P5, * K3, P5; rep from * to last 3 sts, K3.

ROW 5: K1, P3, K4, * P4, K4; rep from * to last 2 sts, P1, K1.

ROW 6: * K2, P3, K2, P1; rep from * to last 2 sts, K2.

ROW 7: K1, P1, * K2, P2; rep from * to last 4 sts, K2, P1, K1.

ROW 8: * K2, P1, K2, P3; rep from *

to last 2 sts, K2.

ROW 9: K1, P1, K4, * P4, K4; rep from * to last 4 sts, P3, K1.

ROW 10: * K3, P5; rep from * to last 2 sts, K2.

ROW 11: Rep Row 3.

ROW 12: * K2, P6; rep from * to last 2 sts, K2.

Rep Rows 3–12 three times more, ending with a Row 12.

Rep Rows 1 & 2 once more. BO.

MIX-AND-MATCH

26 Sextet

Special techniques

Working color patterns by the intarsia method

Using yarn A, CO 33 sts. Starting at the bottom right-hand corner of the chart, work the 42-row pattern, reading odd-numbered rows (right side rows—K all sts) from right to left and even-numbered rows (wrong side rows—P all sts) from left to right. BO.

MIX-AND-MATCH

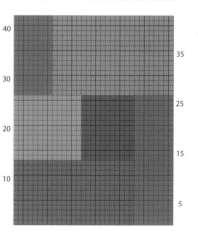

YARN A   YARN B

YARN C   YARN D   YARN E   YARN F

27 Double Cable

Special technique
Working cables

Special abbreviations

C6B = slip next 3 sts onto cable needle, hold at back of work, knit next 3 sts from left-hand needle, then knit stitches from cable needle.

C6F = slip next 3 sts onto cable needle, hold at front of work, knit next 3 sts from left-hand needle, then knit stitches from cable needle.

CO 36 sts.

ROW 1: (RS) K1, P11, K12, P11, K1.

ROW 2: K12, P12, K12.

ROW 3: K1, P11, C6B, C6F, P11, K1.

ROW 4: Rep Row 2.

ROW 5: Rep Row 1.

ROW 6: K12, P12, K12.

Rep Rows 1–6 six times more, ending with a Row 6.

BO.

MIX-AND-MATCH

 50

 126

 161

28 Flapover

After blocking, overlap ribbed edge of top section over bottom section and pin in place to make a 6-in (15-cm) square. Stitch side edges together. Position buttons evenly across rib and stitch in place through both layers.

BUTTONS: 4 metal buttons approximately ⅝ in (16 mm) in diameter

Top section

Using yarn A, CO 34 sts.

ROW 1: (RS) * K2, P2; rep from * to last 2 sts, K2.

ROW 2: K1, P1, * K2, P2; rep from * to last 4 sts, K2, P1, K1.

Rep Rows 1 & 2 three times more, ending with a Row 2.

ROW 9: Knit.

ROW 10: K1, P to last st, K1.

Rep Rows 9 & 10 nine times more, ending with a Row 10.

Rep Row 9 once more. BO.

Bottom section

Using yarn B, CO 34 sts.

ROW 1: (RS) Knit.

ROW 2: K1, P to last st, K1.

Rep Rows 1 & 2 twelve times more. BO.

MIX-AND-MATCH

 26

 85

 157

29 Humbug

Special technique
Working lace patterns

NOTE At color changes, don't break off yarn, but carry color not in use up side of work.

Using yarn A, CO 34 sts.

ROW 1: (RS) Using yarn A, K.

ROW 2: Using yarn A, K1, * K4, P8, K4; rep from * to last st, K1.

ROW 3: Using yarn B, K1, * P3, K2tog, K3, YO, K3, sl 1, K1, psso, P3; rep from * to last st, K1.

ROW 4: Using yarn B, K1, * K3, P4, P into front and back of YO made on previous row, P4, K3; rep from * to last st, K1.

ROW 5: Using yarn A, K1, * P2, K2tog, K3, YO, K2, YO, K3, sl 1, K1, psso, P2; rep from * to last st, K1.

ROW 6: Using yarn A, K1, * K2, P12, K2; rep from * to last st, K1.

ROW 7: Using yarn B, K1, * P1, K2tog, K3, YO, K4, YO, K3, sl 1,

psso, P1; rep from * to last st, K1.

ROW 8: Using yarn B, K1, * K1, P14, K1; rep from * to last st, K1.

ROW 9: Using yarn A, K1, * K2tog, K3, YO, K6, YO, K3, sl 1, K1, psso; rep from * to last st, K1.

ROW 10: Using yarn A, K1, P to last st, K1.

Rep Rows 1–10 three times more, working alternate two-row stripes of color and ending with a Row 10.

Rep Rows 1 & 2 once more.

BO.

MIX-AND-MATCH

30 Abstract

Special techniques
Working color patterns by the intarsia method

Using yarn A, CO 33 sts.

ROW 1: (WS) Using yarn A, K.

ROWS 2–5: Knit.

ROW 6: K12 in yarn A, K21 in yarn B.

ROW 7: P21 in yarn B, P12 in yarn A.

Rep Rows 6 & 7 five times more, ending with a Row 7.

ROWS 18–23: Using yarn A, K.

ROWS 24 & 25: Using yarn C, K.

ROW 26: K19 in yarn C, K14 in

yarn D.

ROW 27: P14 in yarn D, P19 in yarn A.

Rep Rows 26 & 27 four times more, ending with a Row 27.

ROWS 38–43: Using yarn C, K.

ROW 44: Using yarn B, K.

ROW 45: Using yarn B, P.

Rep Rows 44 & 45 once more.

ROWS 48–53: Using yarn D, K.

BO.

MIX-AND-MATCH

31 Seeded Diamonds

CO 33 sts.
ROW 1: (RS) Knit.
ROW 2: K1, * P7, K1; rep from * to end.
ROW 3: K4, * P1, K7; rep from * to last 5 sts, P1, K4.
ROW 4: K1, * P2, K1, P1, K1, P2, K1; rep from * to end.
ROW 5: K2, * [P1, K1] twice, P1, K3; rep from * to last 7 sts, [P1, K1] twice, P1, K2.
ROW 6: Rep Row 4.
ROW 7: Rep Row 3.
ROW 8: K1, * P7, K1; rep from * to end.
Rep Rows 1–8 five times more,
ending with a Row 8.
Rep Row 1 once more.
BO.

MIX-AND-MATCH

 45 127 195

32 Loop Stripes

Special technique
Working slip-stitch color patterns

NOTE Slip all stitches purlwise. At color changes, don't break off yarn, but carry color not in use up side of work.
Using yarn A, CO 37 sts.
ROW 1: (RS) Using yarn A, K.
ROW 2: Using yarn A, K1, P to last st, K1.
ROWS 3 & 4: Using yarn B, K1, * sl 1 with yarn at back, K1; rep from * to end.
ROW 5: Using yarn B, K.
ROW 6: Using yarn B, K1, P to last st, K1.
ROW 7: Using yarn A, K2, sl 1 with yarn at back, * K1, sl 1 with yarn at back; rep from * to last 2 sts, K2.
ROW 8: Using yarn A, K2, * sl 1 with yarn at back, K1; rep from * to last st, K1.
Rep Rows 1–8 seven times more, ending with a Row 8.
Rep Rows 1 & 2 once more. BO.

MIX-AND-MATCH

 48 62 121

33 Lace Leaf

Special technique
Working lace patterns

CO 33 sts.
ROW 1: (RS) Knit.
ROW 2 AND EVERY ALT ROW: K1, P to last st, K1.
ROW 3: K4, K2tog, YO, K1, YO, sl 1, K1, psso, * K5, K2tog, YO, K1, YO, sl 1, K1, psso; rep from * to last 4 sts, K4.
ROW 5: K3, K2tog, YO, K3, YO, sl 1, K1, psso, * K3, K2tog, YO, K3, YO, sl 1, K1, psso; rep from * to last 3 sts, K3.
ROWS 7 & 9: Rep Row 3.
ROW 11: Knit.
ROW 13: K2, * YO, sl 1, K1, psso, K5, K2tog, YO, K1; rep from * to last st, K1.
ROW 15: K3, YO, sl 1, K1, psso, K3, K2tog, YO, * K3, YO, sl 1, K1, psso, K3, K2tog, YO; rep from * to last 3 sts, K3.

ROWS 17 & 19: Rep Row 13.
ROW 20: K1, P to last st, K1.
Rep Rows 1–20 once more, ending with a Row 20.
Rep Row 1 once more.
BO.

MIX-AND-MATCH

 97   98   174

34 Allsorts

A B C D E F

Special technique
Double decreasing

NOTE When introducing a stripe color, don't break off yarn A. Instead, carry the yarn loosely up the side of the work while knitting with the contrast colors.
Using yarn A, CO 61 sts and K 1 row.
Join yarn B.
ROW 1: (RS) K29, sl 1, K2tog, psso, K29.
ROW 2: Knit.
ROW 3: K28, sl 1, K2tog, psso, K28.
ROW 4: Knit.
ROW 5: K27, sl 1, K1, psso, K27.
ROW 6: Knit.
Break off yarn B.
ROW 7: Using yarn A, K26, sl 1, K1, psso, K26.
ROW 8: Using yarn A, K1, P to last st, K1.
Join yarn C and cont working in

this way, dec 2 sts at center of every RS (odd-numbered) row and working stripes by foll this color sequence:
ROWS 9–14 in yarn C.
ROW 15 in yarn A.
ROW 16: Using yarn A, rep Row 8.
ROWS 17–22 in yarn D.
ROW 23 in yarn A.
ROW 24: Using yarn A, rep Row 8.
ROWS 25–30 in yarn E.
ROW 31 in yarn A.
ROW 32: Using yarn A, rep Row 8.
ROWS 33–38 in yarn B.
ROW 39 in yarn A.
ROW 40: Using yarn A, rep Row 8.
ROWS 41–46 in yarn F.
ROW 47: Using yarn A, K6, sl 1, K2tog, psso, K6.
ROW 48: K.
Cont working in this way, dec 2 sts at center of every RS (odd-numbered) row, using yarn A only, until 3 sts rem on needle, ending with a WS row.
NEXT ROW: K3tog.
Fasten off yarn.

MIX-AND-MATCH

 35   72   92

35 Eyelets

Special technique
Working lace patterns

CO 34 sts.
ROW 1: (RS) Knit.
ROW 2 AND EVERY ALT ROW: K1, P to last st, K1.
Rep Rows 1 & 2 twice more, ending with a Row 2.
ROW 7: K3, * K2tog, YO, K3; rep from * to last st, K1.
ROW 8: K1, P to last st, K1.
Rep Rows 3–8 five times more, ending with a Row 8.
Rep Rows 1 & 2 twice more, ending with a Row 2.

Rep Row 1 once more.
BO.

MIX-AND-MATCH

 34
 141
 212

36 Mock Houndstooth

Special technique
Working slip-stitch color patterns

NOTE Slip all slipped stitches purlwise, keeping yarn on wrong side of work. At color changes, don't break off yarn, but carry color not in use up side of work.
Using yarn A, CO 35 sts.
ROW 1: (RS) Using yarn A, K1, * sl 1, K2; rep from * to last st, K1.
ROW 2: Using yarn A, K1, P to last st, K1.
ROW 3: Using yarn B, K1, * K2, sl 1; rep from * to last st, K1.

ROW 4: Using yarn B, K1, P to end, K1.
Rep Rows 1–4 eleven times more, ending with a Row 4.
Rep Rows 1 & 2 once more.
NEXT ROW: Using yarn A, K.
BO.

MIX-AND-MATCH

 17
 19
 193

37 Little Cables

Special technique
Working cables

Special abbreviation
C4B = slip next 2 sts onto cable needle, hold at back of work, knit next 2 sts from left-hand needle, then knit stitches from cable needle.

CO 44 sts.
ROW 1: (RS) K1, P1, * K4, P2; rep from * to last 6 sts, K4, P1, K1.
ROW 2: K2, * P4, K2; rep from * to end.
ROW 3: K1, P1, * C4B, P2; rep from * to last 6 sts, C4B, P1, K1.
ROW 4: K2, * P4, K2; rep from * to end.
Rep Rows 1–4 ten times more, ending with a Row 4.
BO.

MIX-AND-MATCH

 122
 183
 187

38 Banded Leaf

 A B C D E

Special abbreviation
M1 = make an extra stitch at beginning of row by working yarn over before knitting first stitch on needle.
Using yarn A, CO 3 sts.
ROW 1: M1, K3.
ROW 2: M1, K4.
ROW 3: M1, K2, YO, K1, YO, K2.
ROW 4: M1, K2, P3, K3.
ROW 5: M1, K4, YO, K1, YO, K4.
ROW 6: M1, K3, P5, K4.
ROW 7: M1, K6, YO, K1, YO, K6.
ROW 8: M1, K4, P7, K5.
ROW 9: M1, K8, YO, K1, YO, K8.
ROW 10: M1, K5, P9, K6.
ROW 11: M1, K10, YO, K1, YO, K10.
ROW 12: M1, K6, P11, K7.
ROW 13: M1, K12, YO, K1, YO, K12.
ROW 14: M1, K7, P13, K8.
ROW 15: M1, K14, YO, K1, YO, K14.
ROW 16: M1, K8, P15, K9.
ROW 17: M1, K9, sl 1, K1, psso, K11, K2tog, K9.
ROW 18: M1, K9, P13, K10.
ROW 19: M1, K10, sl 1, K1, psso, K9, K2tog, K10.
ROW 20: M1, K10, P11, K11.
ROW 21: M1, K11, sl 1, K1, psso, K7, K2tog, K11.
ROW 22: M1, K11, P9, K12.
ROW 23: M1, K12, sl 1, K1, psso, K5, K2tog, K12.
ROW 24: M1, K12, P7, K13.
ROW 25: M1, K13, sl 1, K1, psso, K3, K2tog, K13.
ROW 26: M1, K13, P5, K14.
ROW 27: M1, K14, sl 1, K1, psso, K1, K2tog, K14.
ROW 28: M1, K14, P3, K15.
ROW 29: M1, K15, K3tog, K15.
ROWS 30–38: M1, K to end (41 sts).
Break yarn A; join yarn B.
ROW 39: K2 tog, K39.
ROW 40: K2 tog, K38.
Cont dec 1 st in this way, at the same time work stripes of color in the following sequence:
2 rows in yarn C, 2 rows in yarn B, 2 rows in yarn C, 6 rows in yarn D, 2 rows in yarn E, 2 rows in yarn D.
Break yarn D; join yarn A.
Using yarn A, cont dec 1 st in this way until 4 sts rem on needle.
NEXT ROW: K2tog twice. BO.

MIX-AND-MATCH

 40
 108
 181

39 Morse Code

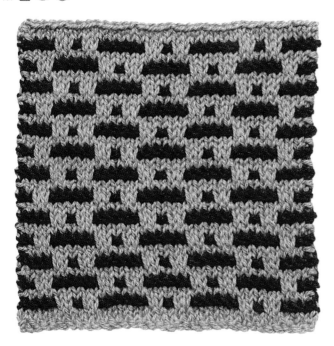

40 Deepdale

ROW 16: K1, * K5, P6; rep from * to last st, K1.
ROWS 17 & 18: Rep Row 16.
ROW 19: Rep Row 15.
ROW 20: Rep Row 14.
ROW 21: Rep Row 13.
ROW 22: Rep Row 12.
Rep Rows 1–22 once more.
BO.

CO 35 sts.
ROW 1: (RS) K1, * P1, K10; rep from * to last st, K1.
ROW 2: K1, * P9, K2; rep from * to last st, K1.
ROW 3: K1, * P3, K8; rep from * to last st, K1.
ROW 4: K1, * P7, K4; rep from * to last st, K1.
ROW 5: K1, * P5, K6; rep from * to last st, K1.
ROWS 6 & 7: Rep Row 5.
ROW 8: Rep Row 4.
ROW 9: Rep Row 3.
ROW 10: Rep Row 2.
ROW 11: Rep Row 1.
ROW 12: K1, * K1, P10; rep from * to last st, K1.
ROW 13: K1, * K9, P2; rep from * to last st, K1.
ROW 14: K1, * K3, P8; rep from * to last st, K1.
ROW 15: K1, * K7, P4; rep from * to last st, K1.

Special technique
Working slip-stitch color patterns

NOTE Slip all stitches purlwise, keeping yarn on wrong side of work. At color changes, don't break off yarn, but carry color not in use up side of work.
Using yarn A, CO 33 sts.
ROW 1: (RS) Using yarn A, K.
ROW 2: Using yarn A, K1, P to last st, K1.
ROWS 3 & 4: Using yarn B, K4, * sl 2, K1, sl 2, K5; rep from * to last 9 sts, sl 2, K1, sl 2, K4.

ROWS 5 & 6: Using yarn A, rep Rows 1 & 2.
ROWS 7 & 8: Using yarn B, K2, sl 2, * K5, sl 2, K1, sl 2; rep from * to last 9 sts, K5, sl 2, K2.
Rep Rows 1–8 five times more, ending with a Row 8.
Rep Rows 1–6 once more.
BO.

MIX-AND-MATCH

 75 114 191

MIX-AND-MATCH

 31 96 191

41 River

Using yarn A, CO 33 sts.
ROW 1: (WS) Knit.
Rep Row 1 four times more.
Break off yarn A; join yarn B.
Rep Row 1 twice more.
Break off yarn B; join yarn C.
ROW 8: Knit.
ROW 9: K1, P to last st, K1.
Rep Rows 8 & 9 sixteen times
more, ending with a Row 9.
Break off yarn C; join yarn B.
Rep Row 1 twice more.
Break off yarn B; join yarn A.
Rep Row 1 six times more.
BO.

MIX-AND-MATCH

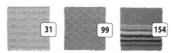

42 Staircase

CO 34 sts.
ROW 1: (RS) * K4, P4; rep from * to
last 2 sts, K2.
ROW 2: K1, P1, * K4, P4; rep from *
to last 8 sts, K4, P3, K1.
ROWS 3 & 4: Rep Rows 1 & 2.
ROW 5: K2, * P4, K4; rep from *
to end.
ROW 6: K1, P3, K4, * P4, K4; rep
from * to last 2 sts, P1, K1.
ROWS 7 & 8: Rep Rows 5 & 6.
ROW 9: K1, P3, K4, * P4, K4; rep
from * to last 2 sts, P1, K1.
ROW 10: K2, * P4, K4; rep from *
to end.
ROWS 11 & 12: Rep Rows 9 & 10.
ROW 13: K1, P1, * K4, P4; rep from
* to last 8 sts, K4, P3, K1.
ROW 14: * K4, P4; rep from * to
last 2 sts, K2.
ROW 15: K1, * K7, P4; rep from *
to last st, K1.
ROW 16: K1, * K5, P6; rep from *

to last st, K1.
Rep Rows 1–16 once more,
ending with a Row 16.
Rep Rows 1–12 once more.
BO.

MIX-AND-MATCH

43 Cable and Rib

Special technique
Working cables

Special abbreviations

C4B = slip next 2 sts onto cable needle, hold at back of work, knit next 2 sts from left-hand needle, then knit stitches from cable needle.

KB1 = knit next stitch through back of loop.

PB1 = purl next stitch through back of loop.

CO 43 sts.

ROW 1: (RS) K1, P2, KB1, P2, * K4, P2, KB1, P2; rep from * to last st, K1.

ROW 2: K3, PB1, K2, * P4, K2, PB1, K2; rep from * to last st, K1.

ROW 3: K1, P2, KB1, P2; * C4B, P2, KB1, P2; rep from * to last st, K1.

ROW 4: K3, PB1, K2, * P4, K2, PB1, K2; rep from * to last st, K1.

Rep Rows 1–4 ten times more, ending with a Row 4.

BO.

MIX-AND-MATCH

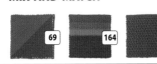

44 Colorful Bobbles

Special technique
Working contrast bobbles

Special abbreviation

MB = make bobble (using contrast yarn, [K1, P1, K1, P1, K1] into next stitch, turn, P5, turn, K5, turn, P2tog, P1, P2tog, turn, sl 1, K2tog, psso. Break off yarn).

Using yarn A, CO 33 sts.

ROW 1: (RS) Knit.

ROW 2 AND EVERY ALT ROW: K1, P to last st, K1.

ROW 3: Knit.

ROW 5: K10, MB in yarn B, K5, MB in yarn C, K5, MB in yarn D, K10.

Cont rep Rows 1 & 2, adding bobbles on the following rows:

ROW 9: K13, MB in yarn B, K5, MB in yarn C, K13.

ROW 13: K10, MB in yarn E, K5, MB in yarn B, K5, MB in yarn C, K10.

ROW 17: K13, MB in yarn E, K5, MB in yarn B, K13.

ROW 21: K10, MB in yarn F, K5, MB in yarn E, K5, MB in yarn B, K10.

ROW 25: K13, MB in yarn F, K5, MB in yarn E, K13.

ROW 29: K10, MB in yarn D, K5, MB in yarn F, K5, MB in yarn E, K10.

ROW 33: K13, MB in yarn D, K5, MB in yarn F, K13.

ROW 37: K10, MB in yarn C, K5, MB in yarn D, K5, MB in yarn F, K10.

ROWS 38 & 40: Rep Row 2.

ROWS 39 & 41: Rep Row 1.

BO.

MIX-AND-MATCH

45 On Point

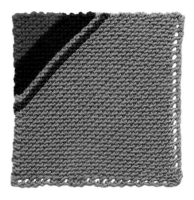

Special technique
Increasing and decreasing

Special abbreviation
INC = increase by knitting into front and back of stitch.

Using yarn A, CO 3 sts and K 1 row.
Begin increase pattern.
ROW 1: (WS) K1, YO, K1, YO, K1.
ROW 2: Knit.
ROW 3: K1, YO, K to last st, YO, K1.
ROW 4: Knit.
Rep Rows 3 & 4 of inc patt until there are 43 sts on needle, ending with a Row 4.
Begin decrease pattern.
ROW 1: K2tog, K to last 2 sts, sl 1, K1, psso.
ROW 2: Knit.
Rep Rows 1 & 2 of dec patt until 27 sts rem on needle, ending with

a Row 2.
Break off yarn A; join yarn B.
Using yarn B, rep Rows 1 & 2 of dec patt once more.
Break off yarn B; join yarn C.
Using yarn C, rep Rows 1 & 2 of dec patt once more.
Break off yarn C; join yarn D.
Using yarn D, rep Rows 1 & 2 of dec patt until 15 sts rem on needle, ending with a Row 2.
Break off yarn D; join yarn E.
Using yarn E, rep Rows 1 & 2 of dec patt until 3 sts rem on needle, ending with a Row 2.
NEXT ROW: K3tog.
Fasten off yarn.

MIX-AND-MATCH

 40 96 191

46 Linked Stripes

Special technique
**Working slip stitch
color patterns**

NOTE Slip all stitches purlwise with yarn at wrong side of work. At color changes, don't break off yarn, but carry color not in use up side of work.

Using yarn A, CO 36 sts.
ROW 1: (RS) Using yarn A, K.
ROW 2: Using yarn A, K.
ROW 3: Using yarn B, K1, * sl 2, K2; rep from * to last 3 sts, sl 2, K1.
ROW 4: Using yarn B, K1, * sl 2, P2; rep from * to last 3 sts, sl 2, K1.
ROWS 5 & 6: Using yarn A, rep Rows 1 & 2.
ROWS 7 & 8: Using yarn B, rep Rows 3 & 4.
ROWS 9 & 10: Using yarn B, K.
ROW 11: Using yarn A, K1, * sl 2,

K2; rep from * to last 3 sts, sl 2, K1.
ROW 12: Using yarn A, K1, * sl 2, P2; rep from * to last 3 sts, sl 2, K1.
ROWS 13 & 14: Using yarn B, K.
ROW 15: Using yarn A, rep Row 11.
ROW 16: Using yarn A, K1, * sl 2, P2; rep from * to last 3 sts, sl 2, K1.
Rep Rows 1–16 three times more, ending with a Row 16.
Rep Row 1 once more.
BO.

MIX-AND-MATCH

 47 77 168

47 Tango

Special technique
Double decreasing

NOTE At color changes on striped block, don't break off yarn, but carry color not in use up side of work.

Striped block

Using yarn A, CO 31 sts and K 1 row.
ROW 1: (RS) K14, sl 1, K2tog, psso, K14.
ROW 2: Knit.
ROW 3: Using yarn B, K13, sl 1, K2tog, psso, K13.
ROW 4: Knit.
Cont working in this way, dec 2 sts at the center of every RS (odd-numbered) row and working two-row stripes in alternate colors until 3 sts remain on the needle, ending with a WS row.
NEXT ROW: K3tog.

Fasten off yarn.

Plain block

CO 31 sts and K 1 row.
ROW 1: (RS) K14, sl 1, K2tog, psso, K14.
ROW 2: Knit.
ROW 3: K13, sl 1, K2tog, psso, K13.
ROW 4: Knit.
Cont working in this way, dec 2 sts at the center of every RS (odd-numbered) row until 3 sts remain on the needle, ending with a WS row.
NEXT ROW: K3tog.
Fasten off yarn.
Make one striped block, one plain block in yarn A, and two plain blocks in yarn C. Using the photograph as a guide to position, join the cast-on edges of the four blocks together using the overcast method of joining shown on page 122.

MIX-AND-MATCH

48 Arched Cables

Special technique
Working cables

Special abbreviations

C4B = slip next 2 sts onto cable needle, hold at back of work, knit next 2 sts from left-hand needle, then knit stitches from cable needle.
C4F = slip next 2 sts onto cable needle, hold at front of work, knit next 2 sts from left-hand needle, then knit stitches from cable needle.

CO 38 sts.
ROW 1: (RS) Knit.
ROW 2 AND EVERY ALT ROW: K1, P to last st, K1.
ROW 3: K1, * C4B, K4, C4F; rep from * to last st, K1.
ROW 5: Knit.
ROW 7: K3, C4F, C4B, * K4, C4F, C4B; rep from * to last 3 sts, K3.
ROW 8: K1, P to last st, K1.
Rep Rows 1–8 four times more, ending with a Row 8.
Rep Rows 1–5 once more.
BO.

MIX-AND-MATCH

St. Ives

CO 34 sts.

ROW 1: (RS) Knit.

ROWS 2 & 3: Rep Row 1.

ROW 4: K2, * P2, K2; rep from * to end.

ROW 5: Knit.

ROWS 6 & 7: Rep Rows 4 & 5.

ROWS 8 & 9: Knit.

ROW 10: K1, P to last st, K1.

Rep Rows 1–10 four times more.

BO.

MIX-AND-MATCH

Crystal Sparkle

  x 22

Special technique
Applying beads with slip stitch

Special abbreviations
M1 = make an extra stitch at beginning of row by working yarn over before knitting first stitch on needle.

B = bead (bring yarn to front of work, slip next stitch, slide bead down close to work, take yarn to back of work).

NOTE Before casting on, thread 22 beads onto yarn. Slip all stitches purlwise.

Using yarn A, CO 3 sts.

ROW 1: M1, K3.

ROW 2: M1, K4.

ROW 3: M1, K2, YO, K1, YO, K2.

ROW 4: M1, K2, P3, K3.

ROW 5: M1, K4, YO, K1, YO, K4.

ROW 6: M1, K3, P5, K4.

ROW 7: M1, K6, YO, K1, YO, K6.

ROW 8: M1, K4, P7, K5.

ROW 9: M1, K8, YO, K1, YO, K8.

ROW 10: M1, K5, P9, K6.

ROW 11: M1, K10, YO, K1, YO, K10.

ROW 12: M1, K6, P11, K7.

ROW 13: M1, K12, YO, K1, YO, K12.

ROW 14: M1, K7, P13, K8.

ROW 15: M1, K14, YO, K1, YO, K14.

ROW 16: M1, K8, P15, K9.

ROW 17: M1, K9, sl 1, K1, psso, K11, K2tog, K9.

ROW 18: M1, K9, P13, K10.

ROW 19: M1, K10, sl 1, K1, psso, K9, K2tog, K10.

ROW 20: M1, K10, P11, K11.

ROW 21: M1, K11, sl 1, K1, psso, K7, K2tog, K11.

ROW 22: M1, K11, P9, K12.

ROW 23: M1, K12, sl 1, K1, psso, K5, K2tog, K12.

ROW 24: M1, K12, P7, K13.

ROW 25: M1, K13, sl 1, K1, psso, K3, K2tog, K13.

ROW 26: M1, K13, P5, K14.

ROW 27: M1, K14, sl 1, K1, psso, K1, K2tog, K14.

ROW 28: M1, K14, P3, K15.

ROW 29: M1, K15, K3tog, K15.

ROWS 30 & 31: M1, K to end.

ROW 32: M1, K1, P to last st, K1.

ROW 33: M1, K3, * B, K3; rep from * to end.

ROWS 34, 35 & 37: Rep Row 32.

ROW 36 & 38: M1, K to end.

ROW 39: K2tog, K to end.

ROW 40: K2tog, P to last st, K1.

ROW 41: K2tog, K3, * B, K3; rep from * to last 2 sts, K2.

ROWS 42, 43 & 45: Rep Row 40.

ROWS 44, 46 & 47: K2tog, K to end.

ROWS 48, 50 & 51: Rep Row 40.

ROW 49: K2tog, K3, * B, K3; rep from * to last 2 sts, K2.

ROW 52: K2tog, K to end.

Rep Row 52 until 4 sts rem on needle, ending with a WS row.

NEXT ROW: K2tog twice.

BO.

MIX-AND-MATCH

51 Arrowheads

52 Block Checkers

CO 33 sts and P 1 row, K 1 row.

ROW 1: (RS) K1, P5, * K1, P9; rep from * to last 7 sts, K1, P5, K1.

ROW 2: K6, * P1, K9; rep from * to last 7 sts, P1, K6.

ROW 3: K1, P4, * K3, P7; rep from * to last 8 sts, K3, P4, K1.

ROW 4: K5, * P3, K7; rep from * to last 8 sts, P3, K5.

ROW 5: K1, P3, * K5, P5; rep from * to last 9 sts, K5, P3, K1.

ROW 6: K4, * P5, K5; rep from * to last 9 sts, P5, K4.

ROW 7: K1, P2, * K7, P3; rep from * to last 10 sts, K7, P2, K1.

ROW 8: K3, * P7, K3; rep from *

to end.

ROW 9: K1, P1, * K9, P1; rep from * to last st, K1.

ROW 10: K2, * P9, K1; rep from * to last st, K1.

Rep Rows 1–10 three times more, ending with a Row 10.

K one row, P one row.

BO.

MIX-AND-MATCH

  21 135 211

Special technique
Working slip-stitch color patterns

NOTE Slip all stitches purlwise, keeping yarn on wrong side of work. At color changes, don't break off yarn, but carry color not in use up side of work.

Using yarn A, CO 34 sts.

- **ROW 1**: (RS) Using yarn A, K.

ROW 2: Using yarn A, K1, P to last st, K1.

ROW 3: Using yarn B, K2, * sl 2, K2; rep from * to end.

ROW 4: Using yarn B, K1, P1, * sl 2, P2; rep from * to last 4 sts, sl 2, P1, K1.

Rep Rows 1–4 thirteen times more, ending with a Row 4.

Rep Rows 1 & 2 once more.

BO.

MIX-AND-MATCH

  106 126 161

53 Framed Square

   A **B**

Special technique
Double decreasing

Using yarn A, CO 31 sts and K 1 row.
ROW 1: (RS) K14, sl 1, K2tog, psso, K14.
ROW 2: Knit.
Break off yarn A; join yarn B.
ROW 3: K13, sl 1, K2tog, psso, K13.

ROW 4: Knit.
Cont working in this way, dec 2 sts at center of every RS (odd-numbered) row until 3 sts rem on the needle, ending with a WS row.
NEXT ROW: K3tog.
Fasten off yarn.
Make three more identical blocks. Using the photograph as a guide to position, join the four blocks together using the overcast method of joining shown on page 122.

MIX-AND-MATCH

54 Pink Flashes

 A **B**

Special technique
Working Fair Isle patterns

Using yarn A, CO 37sts. Starting at the bottom right-hand corner of the chart, work the 42-row pattern, reading odd-numbered rows (right side rows—K all sts) from right to left and even-numbered rows (wrong side rows —P all sts) from left to right. BO.

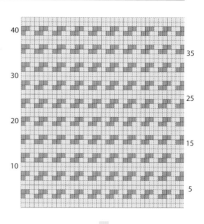

YARN A

YARN B

MIX-AND-MATCH

55 Polperro

CO 34 sts.

ROW 1: (RS) Knit.

ROW 2: K1, P3, K2, * P4, K2; rep from * to last 4 sts, P3, K1.

ROWS 3 & 4: Rep Rows 1 & 2.

ROWS 5 & 7: Knit.

ROW 6: K1, P to last st, K1.

ROW 8: K1, P to last st, K1.

Rep Rows 1–8 four times more, ending with a Row 8.

Rep Rows 1–5 once more.

BO.

MIX-AND-MATCH

 104 113 193

56 Big Heart

Special technique
Working color patterns by the intarsia method

Using yarn A, CO 33 sts. Starting at the bottom right-hand corner of the chart, work the 42-row pattern, reading odd-numbered rows (right side rows—K all sts) from right to left and even-numbered rows (wrong side rows—P all sts) from left to right. BO.

YARN A   YARN B

MIX-AND-MATCH

54   98   113

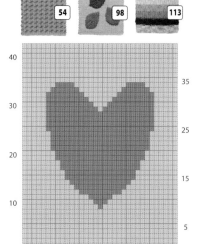

57 Holiday Stripes

58 Snowflake Lace

Special technique
Double decreasing

Using yarn A, CO 61 sts and K 1 row.

ROW 1: (RS) K29, sl 1, K2tog, psso, K29.

ROW 2: Knit.

ROW 3: K28, sl 1, K2tog, psso, K28.

ROWS 4, 6 & 8: Knit.

ROW 5: K27, sl 1, K2tog, psso, K27.

ROW 7: K26, sl 1, K2tog, psso, K26.

ROW 9: K25, sl 1, K2tog, psso, K25.

ROW 10: Knit.

Break off yarn A; join yarn B. Cont working in this way, dec 2 sts

at center of every RS (odd-numbered) row and working contrast stripes by foll this color sequence:

ROWS 11–22: yarn B.

ROWS 23–34: yarn C

Cont in yarn B only, until 3 sts rem on needle, ending with a WS row.

NEXT ROW: K3tog.

Fasten off yarn.

MIX-AND-MATCH

Special technique
Working lace patterns

CO 33 sts.

ROW 1 AND EVERY ALT ROW: (WS) K1, P to last st, K1.

ROW 2: K6, sl 1, K1, psso, YO, K1, YO, K2tog, * K3, sl 1, K1, psso, YO, K1, YO, K2tog; rep from * to last 6 sts, K6.

ROW 4: K7, YO, sl 2, K1, p2sso, YO, * K5, YO, sl 2, K1, p2sso, YO; rep from * to last 7 sts, K7.

ROW 6: Rep Row 2.

ROW 8: K2, sl 1, K1, psso, YO, K1, YO, K2tog, * K3, sl 1, K1, psso, YO,

K1, YO, K2tog; rep from * to last 2 sts, K2.

ROW 10: K3, YO, sl 2, K1, p2sso, YO, * K5, YO, sl 2, K1, p2sso, YO; rep from * to last 3 sts, K3.

ROW 12: K2, sl 1, K1, psso, YO, K1, YO, K2tog, * K3, sl 1, K1, psso, YO, K1, YO, K2tog; rep from * to last 2 sts, K2.

Rep Rows 1–12 twice more, ending with a Row 12.

Rep Rows 1–7 once more. BO.

MIX-AND-MATCH

59 Beaded Tree

ROW 21: K9, B, K13, B, K9.
ROW 23: K10, B, K11, B, K10.
ROW 25: K11, B, K9, B, K11.
ROW 27: K12, B, K7, B, K12.
ROW 29: K13, B, K5, B, K13.
ROW 31: K14, B, K3, B, K14.
ROW 33: K15, B, K1, B, K15.
ROW 35: K16, B, K16.
ROWS 37 & 39: Rep Row 1.
ROW 41: Knit.
ROW 42: K1, P to last st, K1.
BO.

Special technique
Applying beads with slip stitch

Special abbreviation
B = bead (bring yarn to front of work, slip next stitch, slide bead down yarn close to work, take yarn to back of work).

NOTE Before casting on, thread 31 beads onto yarn. Slip all stitches purlwise.
CO 33 sts.
ROW 1: (RS) Knit.
ROW 2 AND EVERY ALT ROW: K1, P to last st, K1.
ROWS 3 & 5: Rep Row 1.
ROWS 7, 9 & 11: K16, B, K16.
ROW 13: K5, [B, K3] twice, [B, K2] twice, [B, K3] twice, B, K5.
ROW 15: K6, B, K19, B, K6.
ROW 17: K7, B, K17, B, K7.
ROW 19: K8, B, K15, B, K8.

60 Candy Cane

ROW 10: Using yarn A, K3, * P6, K6; rep from * to last 9 sts, K6, K3.
ROW 11: Using yarn B, P2, * K6, P6; rep from * to last 10 sts, K6, P4.
ROW 12: Using yarn B, K5, * P6, K6; rep from * to last 7 sts, P6, K1.
Rep Rows 1–12 twice more, ending with a Row 12.
Rep Rows 1–6 once again.
BO.

NOTE At color changes, don't break off yarn, but carry color not in use up side of work.

Using yarn A, CO 36 sts.
ROW 1: (RS) Using yarn A, * K6, P6; rep from * to end.
ROW 2: Using yarn A, P1, * K6, P6; rep from * to last 11 sts, K6, P5.
ROW 3: Using yarn B, K4, * P6, K6; rep from * to last 8 sts, P6, K2.
ROW 4: Using yarn B, P3, * K6, P6; rep from * to last 9 sts, K6, P3.
ROW 5: Using yarn A, K2, * P6, K6; rep from * to last 10 sts, P6, K4.
ROW 6: Using yarn A, P5, * K6, P6; rep from * to last 7 sts, K6, P1.
ROW 7: Using yarn B, * P6, K6; rep from * to end.
ROW 8: Using yarn B, K1, * P6, K6; rep from * to last 11 sts, P6, K5.
ROW 9: Using yarn A, P4, * K6, P6; rep from * to last 8 sts, K6, P2.

MIX-AND-MATCH

 57
 58
 60

MIX-AND-MATCH

 57
 58
 59

61 Elsie's Rose Leaf

Special technique
Working yarn overs

CO 2 sts.
ROW 1: (RS) K1, YO, K1.
ROWS 2, 4 & 6: K1, P to last st, K1.
ROW 3: (K1, YO) twice, K1.
ROW 5: (K1, YO) 4 times, K1.
ROW 7: K1, YO, P1, K2, YO, K1, YO, K2, P1, YO, K1.
ROW 8: K1, P1, K1, P7, K1, P1, K1.
ROW 9: K1, YO, P2, K3, YO, K1, YO, K3, P2, YO, K1.
ROW 10: K1, P1, K2, P9, K2, P1, K1.
ROW 11: K1, YO, P3, K4, YO, K1, YO, K4, P3, YO, K1.
ROW 12: K1, P1, K3, P11, K3, P1, K1.
ROW 13: K1, YO, P4, K5, YO, K1, YO,

K5, P4, YO, K1.
ROW 14: K1, P1, K4, P13, K4, P1, K1.
ROW 15: K1, YO, P5, K6, YO, K1, YO, K6, P5, YO, K1.
ROW 16: K1, P1, K5, P15, K5, P1, K1.
ROW 17: K1, YO, P6, sl 1, K1, psso, K11, K2tog, P6, YO, K1.
ROW 18: K1, P1, K6, P13, K6, P1, K1.
ROW 19: K1, YO, P7, sl 1, K1, psso, K9, K2tog, P7, YO, K1.
ROW 20: K1, P1, K7, P11, K7, P1, K1.
ROW 21: K1, YO, P8, sl 1, K1, psso, K7, K2tog, P8, YO, K1.
ROW 22: K1, P1, K8, P9, K8, P1, K1.
ROW 23: K1, YO, P9, sl 1, K1, psso, K5, K2tog, P9, YO, K1.
ROW 24: K1, P1, K9, P7, K9, P1, K1.
ROW 25: K1, YO, P10, sl 1, K1, psso, K3, K2tog, P10, YO, K1.
ROW 26: K1, P1, K10, P5, K10, P1, K1.
ROW 27: K1, YO, P11, sl 1, K1, psso, K1, K2tog, P11, YO, K1.
ROW 28: K1, P1, K11, P3, K11, P1, K1.
ROW 29: K1, YO, P12, sl 1, K2tog, psso, P12, YO, K1.
ROWS 30, 32, 34 & 36: K1, P1, K to last 2 sts, P1, K1.
ROWS 31, 33, 35 & 37: K1, YO, P to last st, YO, K1.
ROWS 38 & 40: K1, P to last st, K1.
ROW 39: K2tog, K to last 2 sts, K2tog.
ROW 41: * K2tog, YO; rep from *

to last 3 sts, K3tog.
ROW 42: Knit.
ROW 43: K2tog, K to last 2 sts, K2tog.
ROWS 44–46: Rep Rows 38–40.
ROW 47: * K2tog, YO; rep from * to last 2 sts, K2tog.
ROWS 48 & 49: Rep Rows 42 & 43.
ROWS 50–55: Rep Rows 38–43.
ROWS 56–61: Rep Rows 44–49.
ROWS 62–67: Rep Rows 38–43.
ROWS 68–73: Rep Rows 38–43.
ROWS 74–76: Rep Rows 38–40.
ROW 77: K2tog, K1, K2tog.
ROW 78: P3tog.
Fasten off yarn.

MIX-AND-MATCH

 93
 144
 205

62 Interwoven

CO 34 sts.
ROW 1: (RS) Knit.
ROW 2: K1, P to last st, K1.
ROW 3: K2, * P2, K2; rep from * to end.
ROW 4: K1, P1, * K2, P2; rep from * to last 4 sts, K2, P1, K1.
ROWS 5 & 6: Rep Rows 1 & 2.
Row 7: Rep Row 4.
ROW 8: K2, * P2, K2; rep from * to end.
Rep Rows 1–8 four times more, ending with a Row 8.
Rep Rows 1–6 once again.
BO.

MIX-AND-MATCH

 138
 163
 185

63 Toffee Stripes

Using yarn A, CO 33 sts.

ROW 1: (RS) K3, * P3, K5; rep from * to last 6 sts, P3, K3.

ROW 2: K1, P2, * K3, P5; rep from * to last 6 sts, K3, P2, K1.

ROW 3: K3, * P1, YO, P2tog, K5; rep from * to last 6 sts, P1, YO, P2tog, K3.

ROW 4: Rep Row 2.

ROW 5: Rep Row 1.

ROW 6: K1, P to last st, K1. Break off yarn A; join yarn B.

ROW 7: K7, * P3, K5; rep from * to last 10 sts, P3, K7.

ROW 8: K1, P6, * K3, P5; rep from * to last 10 sts, K3, P5, K2.

ROW 9: K7, * P1, YO, P2tog, K5; rep from * to last 10 sts, P1, YO, P2tog, K7.

ROW 10: Rep Row 8.

ROW 11: Rep Row 7.

ROW 12: K1, P to last st, K1.

Rep Rows 1–12 twice more, alternating yarn colors every 6 rows and ending with a Row 12. Rep Rows 1–6 once more. BO.

MIX-AND-MATCH

64 Pyramids

NOTE Slip all stitches purlwise. At color changes, don't break off main yarn, but carry it up side of work.

Using yarn A, CO 35 sts.

ROWS 1 & 2: (RS) Using yarn A, K.

ROW 3: Using yarn A, * K3, sl 1; rep from * to last 3 sts, K3.

ROW 4: Using yarn A, * P3, sl 1; rep from * to last 3 sts, P3.

ROW 5: Using yarn B, * K3, sl 1; rep from * to last 3 sts, K3.

ROW 6: Using yarn B, K.

ROW 7: Using yarn A, K1, * sl 1, K3; rep from * to last 2 sts, sl 1, K1.

ROW 8: Using yarn A, P1, * sl 1, P3; rep from * to last 2 sts, sl 1, P1.

ROW 9: Using yarn A, K1, * sl 1, K3; rep from * to last 2 sts, sl 1, K1.

ROW 10: Using yarn A, K.

Rep Rows 3–10 six times more, ending with a Row 10. Rep Rows 3 & 4 once more. Using yarn A, rep Rows 5 & 6 once more.

NEXT ROW: Using yarn A, K. BO.

MIX-AND-MATCH

65 Beaded Square

ROW 13: Rep Row 5.

ROWS 19 & 23: Rep Row 3.

ROW 21: Rep Row 5.

ROWS 25 & 33: Knit.

ROWS 27 & 31: Rep Row 11.

ROW 29: Rep Row 5.

ROWS 35 & 39: Rep Row 3.

ROW 37: Rep Row 5.

ROW 40: Purl.

ROW 41: Knit.

BO.

Special technique
Applying beads with slip stitch

Special abbreviation
B = bead (bring yarn to front of work, slip next stitch, slide bead down yarn close to work, take yarn to back of work).

NOTE Before casting on, thread beads onto yarn in this sequence: 2a, 5b, 4a, 5b, 4a, 5b, 4a, 5b, 4a, 5b, 2a. You will need 20 beads of color a and 25 of color b. Slip all stitches purlwise.

Using yarn A, CO 33 sts.

ROW 1: (RS) Knit.

ROW 2 AND EVERY ALT ROW: Purl.

ROW 3 & 7: K13, B, K5, B, K13.

ROW 5: K4, * B, K5; rep from * to last 5 sts, B, K4.

ROWS 9 & 17: Knit.

ROWS 11 & 15: K7, B, K17, B, K7.

66 Vertical Stripes

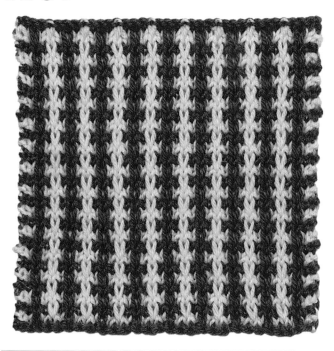

Special technique
Working slip-stitch color patterns

NOTE Slip all stitches purlwise, keeping yarn on wrong side of work. At color changes, don't break off yarn, but carry color not in use up side of work.

Using yarn A, CO 37 sts.

ROW 1: (RS) Using yarn B, K2, * sl 1, K3; rep from * to last 3 sts, K3.

ROW 2: Using yarn B, K1, P1, * sl 1, P3; rep from * to last 3 sts, sl 1, P1, K1.

ROW 3: Using yarn A, K4, * sl 1, K3; rep from * to last st, K1.

ROW 4: Using yarn A, K1, P3, * sl 1, P3; rep from * to last st, K1.

Rep Rows 1–4 twelve times more, ending with a Row 4.

Rep Rows 1–3 once more.

BO.

MIX-AND-MATCH

MIX-AND-MATCH

67 Chevron

CO 33 sts.

ROW 1: (RS) K1, * P7, K1; rep from * to end.

ROW 2: P1, * K7, P1; rep from * to end.

ROW 3: K2, * P5, K3; rep from * to last 7 sts, P5, K2.

ROW 4: P2, * K5, P3; rep from * to last 7 sts, K5, P2.

ROW 5: K3, * P3, K5; rep from * to last 6 sts, P3, K3.

ROW 6: P3, * K3, P5; rep from * to last 6 sts, K3, P3.

ROW 7: K4, * P1, K7; rep from * to last 5 sts, P1, K4.

ROW 8: P4, * K1, P7; rep from * to last 5 sts, K1, P4.

ROW 9: Rep Row 2.

ROW 10: Rep Row 1.

ROW 11: Rep Row 4.

ROW 12: Rep Row 3.

ROW 13: Rep Row 6.

ROW 14: Rep Row 5.

ROW 15: Rep Row 8.

ROW 16: K4, * P1, K7; rep from * to last 5 sts, P1, K4.

Rep Rows 1–16 once more, ending with a Row 16.

Rep Rows 1–10 once more.

BO.

MIX-AND-MATCH

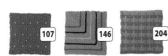

68 Indian Stripe

Special technique
Working Fair Isle patterns

NOTE Wherever possible, don't break off yarn at color changes, but carry colors not in use loosely up side of work.

Using yarn A, CO 34 sts.

ROW 1: (RS) Using yarn A, K.

ROW 2: Using yarn A, K1, P to last st, K1.

ROW 3: Using yarn A, K.

ROW 4: Using yarn B, K1, P to last st, K1.

ROW 5: Using yarn B, K.

ROW 6: Using yarn C, K1, P to last st, K1.

ROW 7: Using yarn B, K.

ROW 8: Using yarn C, K1, P to last st, K1.

ROW 9: Using yarn C, K.

ROW 10: * P1 in yarn C, P1 in yarn B; rep from * to end.

ROW 11: Using yarn B, K.

ROW 12: Using yarn B, K1, P to last st, K1.

ROW 13: * K1 in yarn A, K1 in yarn B; rep from * to end.

ROW 14: Using yarn A, K1, P to last st, K1.

ROW 15: Using yarn A, K.

ROW 16: Using yarn B, K1, P to last st, K1.

ROW 17: Using yarn B, K.

ROW 18: Using yarn C, K1, P to last st, K1.

ROW 19: Using yarn C, K.

ROW 20: * P1 in yarn C, P1 in yarn B; rep from * to end.

ROW 21: Using yarn C, K.

ROW 22: Using yarn C, K1, P to last st, K1.

Rep Rows 21 & 22 ten times more, ending with a Row 22.

BO.

MIX-AND-MATCH

69 Twin Triangles

Special technique
Increasing and decreasing

Using yarn A, CO 3 sts and K
1 row.
Begin increase pattern.
ROW 1: (RS) K1, YO, K1, YO, K1.
ROW 2: Knit.
ROW 3: K1, YO, K to last st, YO, K1.
ROW 4: Knit.
Rep Rows 3 & 4 until there are
43 sts on needle, ending with a
Row 4.
Break off yarn A; join yarn B.
Begin decrease pattern.
NEXT ROW: K2tog, K to last 2 sts,

sl 1, K1, psso.
NEXT ROW: Knit.
Cont rep 2-row dec patt until
3 sts rem on needle, ending with
a Row 2.
NEXT ROW: K3tog.
Fasten off yarn.

MIX-AND-MATCH

70 Interlaced Cables

Special technique
Working cables

Special abbreviations
C6F = slip next 3 sts onto cable
needle, hold at front of work,
knit next 3 sts from left-hand
needle, then knit stitches from
cable needle.
C6B = slip next 3 sts onto cable
needle, hold at back of work,
knit next 3 sts from left-hand
needle, then knit stitches from
cable needle.

CO 35 sts.

ROW 1: (RS) K1, P9, K15, P9, K1.
ROW 2: K10, P15, K10.
ROW 3: K1, P9, K3, * C6F; rep from
* to last 10 sts, P9, K1.
ROW 4: Rep Row 2.
ROWS 5 & 6: Rep Rows 1 & 2.
ROW 7: K1, P9, * C6B; rep from * to
last 13 sts, K3, P9, K1.
ROW 8: K10, P15, K10.
Rep Rows 1–8 five times more,
ending with a Row 8.
BO.

MIX-AND-MATCH

71 Dolly Mixtures

WE A B C

ROW 9: Using yarn C, rep Row 4.
ROW 10: Using yarn C, rep Row 3.
ROW 11: Using yarn A, rep Row 6.
ROW 12: Using yarn A, rep Row 5.
Rep Rows 1–12 five times more,
ending with a Row 12.
Rep Rows 1–6 once more.
BO.

Special technique
Working slip-stitch color patterns

NOTE Slip all stitches purlwise,
with yarn at wrong side of work.
At color changes, don't break off
yarn, but carry colors not in use
up side of work.
Using yarn A, CO 38 sts.
ROW 1: (RS) Using yarn B, K1, * sl
3, K3; rep from * to last st, K1.
ROW 2: Using yarn B, K1, * K3, sl 3;
rep to last st, K1.
ROW 3: Using yarn C, K1, * K3, sl 3;
rep from * to last st, K1.
ROW 4: Using yarn C, K1, * sl 3, K3;
rep from * to last st, K1.
ROW 5: Using yarn A, K1, * sl 3, K3;
rep from * to last st, K1.
ROW 6: Using yarn A, K1, * K3, sl 3;
rep from * to last st, K1.
ROW 7: Using yarn B, rep Row 2.
ROW 8: Using yarn B, rep Row 1.

MIX-AND-MATCH

 83 87 203

72 Zigzag Columns

¥ ≡ ⬤

CO 34 sts and K 1 row.
ROW 1: (RS) K1, P to last st, K1.
ROW 2: Knit.
ROW 3: K1, P1, K4, P2, K2, * P3,
K4, P2, K2; rep from * to last 2 sts,
P1, K1.
ROW 4: K2, * P3, K2, P3, K3; rep
from * to last 10 sts, P3, K2, P3, K2.
ROW 5: K1, P1, K2, P2, K4, * P3,
K2, P2, K4; rep from * to last 2 sts,
P1, K1.
ROW 6: K2, P5, K2, P1, * K3, P5, K2,
P1; rep from * to last 2 sts, K2.
ROW 7: K1, P1, K1, P2, K5, * P3,
K1, P2, K5; rep from * to last 2 sts,
P1, K1.

ROW 8: K2, P4, K2, P2, * K3, P4, K2,
P2; rep from * to last 2 sts, K2.
ROW 9: K1, P1, * K3, P2, K3, P3;
rep from * to last 10 sts, K3, P2, K3,
P1, K1.
ROW 10: K2, P2, K2, P4, * K3, P2,
K2, P4; rep from * to last 2 sts, K2.
Rep Rows 1–10 three times more,
ending with a Row 10.
Rep Rows 1 & 2 once more.
NEXT ROW: K1, P to last st, K1. BO.

MIX-AND-MATCH

 34 88 151

73 Two Edges

Special technique
Double decreasing

Using yarn A, CO 61 sts and K 1 row.
ROW 1: (RS) K29, sl 1, K2tog, psso, K29.
ROW 2: Knit.
ROW 3: K28, sl 1, K2tog, psso, K28.
ROW 4: Knit.
Break off yarn A; join yarn B.
ROW 5: K27, sl 1, K2tog, psso, K27.
ROW 6: Knit.
Break off yarn B; join yarn C.
ROW 7: K26, sl 1, K2tog, psso, K26.
Using yarn C, cont working in this

way, dec 2 sts at center of every RS (odd-numbered) row until until 3 sts rem on needle, ending with a WS row.
NEXT ROW: K3tog.
Fasten off yarn.

MIX-AND-MATCH

 121   123   135

74 Alternate Eyelets

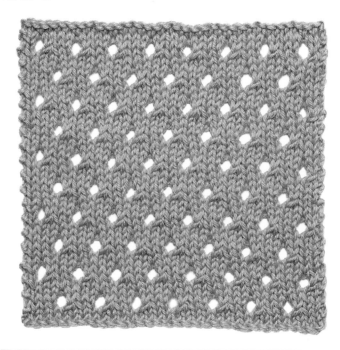

Special technique
Working lace patterns

CO 33 sts.
ROW 1: (RS) Knit.
ROW 2 AND EVERY ALT ROW: K1, P to last st, K1.
ROW 3: K1, * K2, K2tog, YO; rep from * to last 4 sts, K4.
ROW 5: Knit.
ROW 7: K1, * K2tog, YO, K2; rep from * to end.
ROW 8: K1, P to last st, K1.
Rep Rows 1–8 four times more, ending with a Row 8.
Rep Row 1 once more. BO.

MIX-AND-MATCH

 49   119   162

75 Seed Squares

CO 32 sts.

ROW 1: (WS) K1, * P1, K1, P1, K1, P6; rep from * to last st, K1.

ROW 2: K1, * K5, P1, K1, P1, K1, P1; rep from * to last st, K1.

ROWS 3, 5 & 7: Rep Row 1.

ROWS 4, 6 & 8: Rep Row 2.

ROW 9: K1, * P6, K1, P1, K1, P1; rep from * to last st, K1.

ROW 10: K1, * P1, K1, P1, K1, P1, K5; rep from * to last st, K1.

ROWS 11, 13 & 15: Rep Row 9.

ROWS 12 & 14: Rep Row 10.

ROW 16: K1, * P1, K1, P1, K1, P1, K5; rep from * to last st, K1.

Rep Rows 1–16 twice more,

ending with a Row 16.

BO.

MIX-AND-MATCH

 114

 121

 191

76 Eccentric Stripes

Using yarn A, CO 33 sts.

ROW 1: (RS) Knit.

ROW 2: Purl.

Rep Rows 1 & 2, changing yarn in the foll color sequence:

6 rows in yarn A, 2 rows in yarn B,

6 rows in yarn A, 3 rows in yarn C,

1 row in yarn D, 4 rows in yarn C,

2 rows in yarn E, 1 row in yarn C,

5 rows in yarn F, 2 rows in yarn C,

2 rows in yarn B, 6 rows in yarn A.

BO.

MIX-AND-MATCH

 116

 51

 129

77 Blocky

 ⚹ 〓 A B C D E

Special technique
Working color patterns by the intarsia method

Using yarn A, CO 33 sts. Starting at the bottom right-hand corner of the chart, work the 42-row pattern, reading odd-numbered rows (right side rows—K all sts) from right to left and even-numbered rows (wrong side rows—P all sts) from left to right. BO.

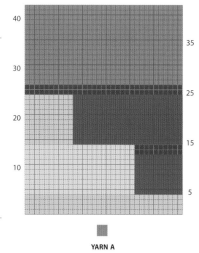

40
35
30
25
20
15
10
5

YARN A

YARN B

YARN C

YARN D

YARN E

MIX-AND-MATCH

 10   11   173

78 Lattice

⚹ 〓 ●

CO 33 sts.
ROW 1: (RS) Knit.
ROW 2: K1, P to last st, K1.
ROWS 3 & 4: Rep Rows 1 & 2.
ROW 5: K1, P2, * K3, P3; rep from * to last 6 sts, K3, P2, K1.
ROW 6: K1, P to last st, K1.
ROWS 7 & 8: Rep Rows 5 & 6.
ROW 9: Rep Row 5.
ROW 10 & 12: Rep Row 2.
ROW 11 & 13: Knit.
ROW 14 & 16: Rep Row 5.
ROW 15 & 17: Knit.
ROW 18: K1, P2, * K3, P3; rep from * to last 6 sts, K3, P2, K1.
Rep Rows 1–18 once more,

ending with a Row 18.
Rep Rows 1–13 once more.
BO.

MIX-AND-MATCH

 96   186   191

79 Ridged Columns

CO 37 sts.

ROW 1 AND EVERY ALT ROW: (RS) K1,
P1, * K5, P2; rep from * to last 7 sts,
K5, P1, K1.

ROW 2: K9, * P5, K9; rep from *
to end.

ROW 4: K2, * P5, K2; rep from *
to end.

ROW 6: K2, P5, * K9, P5; rep from
* to last 2 sts, K2.

ROW 8: K2, * P5, K2; rep from *
to end.

Rep Rows 1–8 four times more,
ending with a Row 8.
Rep Rows 1 & 2 once more.
BO.

MIX-AND-MATCH

80 Buzz

Special technique
Double decreasing

NOTE At color changes, don't
break off yarn, but carry color not
in use up side of work.
Using yarn A, CO 61 sts and K
1 row.

ROW 1: (RS) K29, sl 1, K2tog,
psso, K29.

ROW 2: Knit.
Join yarn B.

ROW 3: K28, sl 1, K2tog, psso, K28.

ROW 4: Knit.

Cont working in this way, dec 2
sts at center of every RS (odd-
numbered) row and working two-
row stripes of alternate colors
until 3 sts rem on needle, ending
with a WS row.

NEXT ROW: K3tog.
Fasten off yarn.
BO.

MIX-AND-MATCH

81 Chevron Eyelets

Special technique
Working lace patterns

CO 31 sts and K 2 rows.
ROW 1: (RS) K2, * K4, YO, sl 1, K1, psso, K3; rep from * to last 2 sts, K2.
ROW 2 AND EVERY ALT ROW: K2, P to last 2 sts, K2.
ROW 3: K2, * K2, K2tog, YO, K1, YO, sl 1, K1, psso, K2; rep from * to last 2 sts, K2.
ROW 5: K2, * K1, K2tog, YO, K3, YO, sl 1, K1, psso, K1; rep from * to last 2 sts, K2.
ROW 7: K2, * K2tog, YO, K5, YO, sl 1,

K1, psso; rep from * to last 2 sts, K2.
ROW 8: K2, P to last st, K2.
Rep Rows 1–8 three times more, ending with a Row 8.
Rep Rows 1–7 once more.
K 2 rows.
BO.

MIX-AND-MATCH

 143 150 176

82 Dash

Special technique
Working slip-stitch color patterns

NOTE Slip all stitches purlwise, keeping yarn on wrong side of work.
Using yarn A, CO 34 sts.
ROW 1: (RS) Using yarn A, K.
ROW 2: Using yarn A, K1, P to last st, K1.
ROWS 3 & 4: Using yarn B, K4, * sl 2, K4; rep from * to end.
ROWS 5 & 6: Using yarn A, rep Rows 1 & 2.
ROW 7: Using yarn C, K1, sl 2, * K4,

sl 2; rep from * to last st, K1.
ROW 8: Using yarn C, K1, sl 2, * K4, sl 2; rep from * to last st, K1.
Rep Rows 1–8 once more, ending with a Row 8.
Rep Rows 1–4 once more.
Cont in patt using yarn A throughout.
Rep Rows 5–8 once more.
Rep Rows 1–8 three times more, ending with a Row 8.
Rep Rows 1–6 once more. BO.

MIX-AND-MATCH

 23 84 116

83 Checks

84 Beaded Leaf

CO 35 sts.

ROW 1: (RS) K4, * P3, K3; rep from * to last st, K1.

ROW 2: K1, P3, * K3, P3; rep from * to last st, K1.

ROWS 3 & 4: Rep Rows 1 & 2.

ROWS 5 & 7: Rep Row 2.

ROW 6: Rep Row 1.

ROW 8: K4, * P3, K3; rep from * to last st, K1.

Rep Rows 1–8 four times more, ending with a Row 8.

Rep Rows 1–4 once more.

BO.

Special technique
Applying beads with slip stitch

Special abbreviations
M1 = make an extra stitch at beginning of row by working yarn over before knitting first stitch on needle.

B = bead (bring yarn to front of work, slip next stitch, slide bead down close to work, take yarn to back of work).

NOTE Before casting on, thread 13 beads onto yarn A. Slip all stitches purlwise.

CO 1 st.

ROW 1: (RS) M1, K1.

ROW 2: M1, K2.

ROW 3: M1, K1, YO, K1, YO, K1.

ROW 4: M1, K1, P3, K2.

ROW 5: M1, K2, YO, K1, B, K1, YO, K2.

ROW 6: M1, K2, P5, K3.

ROW 7: M1, K3, YO, K2, B, K2, YO, K3.

ROW 8: M1, K3, P7, K4.

ROW 9: M1, K4, YO, K3, B, K3, YO, K4.

ROW 10: M1, K4, P9, K5.

ROW 11: M1, K5, YO, K4, B, K4, YO, K5.

ROW 12: M1, K5, P11, K6.

ROW 13: M1, K6, YO, K5, B, K5, YO, K6.

ROW 14: M1, K6, P13, K7.

ROW 15: M1, K7, YO, K6, B, K6, YO, K7.

ROW 16: M1, K7, P15, K8.

ROW 17: M1, K15, B, K15.

ROW 18: M1, K8, P15, K9.

ROW 19: M1, K9, sl 1, K1, psso, K5, B, K5, K2tog, K9.

ROW 20: M1, K9, P13, K10.

ROW 21: M1, K10, sl 1, K1, psso, K4, B, K4, K2tog, K10.

ROW 22: M1, K10, P11, K11.

ROW 23: M1, K11, sl 1, K1, psso, K3, B, K3, K2tog, K11.

ROW 24: M1, K11, P9, K12.

ROW 25: M1, K12, sl 1, K1, psso, K2, B, K2, K2tog, K12.

ROW 26: M1, K12, P7, K13.

ROW 27: M1, K13, sl 1, K1, psso, K1, B, K1, K2tog, K13.

ROW 28: M1, K13, P5, K14.

ROW 29: M1, K14, sl 1, K1, psso, B, K2tog, K14.

ROW 30: M1, K14, P3, K15.

ROW 31: M1, K15, sl 1, K2tog, psso, K15.

ROWS 32–39: M1, K to end.

Break off yarn A; join yarn B.

ROWS 40 & 41: Using yarn B, K to end.

Break off yarn B; join yarn C. Cont in patt using yarn C as folls:

ROW 42: P2tog, P to end.

ROWS 43 & 44: K2tog, K to end.

ROW 45: P2tog, P to end.

Rep Rows 43–45 until 2 sts rem on needle.

BO.

MIX-AND-MATCH

MIX-AND-MATCH

85 Honeycomb

Special technique
Working cables

Special abbreviations

C4B = slip next 2 sts onto cable needle, hold at back of work, knit next 2 sts from left-hand needle, then knit stitches from cable needle.

C4F = slip next 2 sts onto cable needle, hold at front of work, knit next 2 sts from left-hand needle, then knit stitches from cable needle.

CO 36 sts.

ROW 1: (RS) K1, P9, K16, P9, K1.

ROW 2: K10, P16, K10.

ROW 3: K1, P9, [C4B, C4F] twice, P9, K1.

ROW 4: Rep Row 2.

ROWS 5 & 6: Rep Rows 1 & 2.

ROW 7: K1, P9, [C4F, C4B] twice, P9, K1.

ROW 8: K10, P16, K10.

Rep Rows 1–8 five times more, ending with a Row 8. BO.

MIX-AND-MATCH

86 Piazza

Special technique
Working slip-stitch color patterns, working elongated stitches

NOTE Slip all stitches purlwise with yarn at wrong side of work. At color changes, don't break off yarn, but carry color not in use up side of work.

Using yarn A, CO 33 sts.

ROW 1: (RS) Using yarn B, K3, * sl 2, K3; rep from * to end.

ROW 2: Using yarn B, P3, * [P1 winding yarn twice around needle] twice, P3; rep from * to end.

ROW 3: Using yarn A, K3, sl 2 dropping extra loops, K3; rep from * to end.

ROW 4: Using yarn A, K3, * sl 2, K3; rep from * to end.

ROW 5: Using yarn A, K3, * sl 2, K3; rep from * to end.

ROW 6: Using yarn A, P3, * [P1 winding yarn twice around needle] twice, P3; rep from * to end.

ROW 7: Using yarn B, K3, sl 2 dropping extra loops, K3; rep from * to end.

ROW 8: Using yarn B, K3, * sl 2, K3; rep from * to end.

Rep Rows 1–8 five times more, ending with a Row 8.

Rep Rows 1–5 once more.

NEXT ROW: Using yarn B, P. BO.

MIX-AND-MATCH

87 Hot Stripes

Using yarn A, CO 32 sts.

ROW 1: (RS) K1, P3, * K5, P3; rep from * to last 4 sts, K4.

ROW 2: K1, P4, * K3, P5; rep from * to last 3 sts, K3.

ROW 3: K1, P1, K5, * P3, K5; rep from * to last st, K1.

ROW 4: K2, P5, * K3, P5; rep from * to last st, K1.

ROW 5: K5, * P3, K5; rep from * to last 3 sts, P2, K1.

ROW 6: K4, * P5, K3; rep from * to last 4 sts, P3, K1.

ROW 7: K3, P3, * K5, P3; rep from * to last 2 sts, K2.

ROW 8: K1, P2, K3, * P5, K3; rep from * to last 2 sts, K1, P1.

Break off yarn A; join yarn B.

Rep Rows 1–8 once more, ending with a Row 8.

Break off yarn B; join yarn A.

Rep Rows 1–8 three times more, ending with a Row 8.

Rep Rows 1–4 once more.

BO.

MIX-AND-MATCH

 10 132 151

88 Shutter

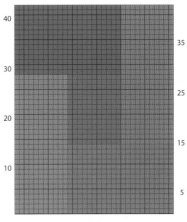

Special technique
Working color patterns by the intarsia method

Using yarn A, CO 33 sts.
Starting at the bottom right-hand corner of the chart, work the 42-row pattern, reading odd-numbered rows (right side rows —K all sts) from right to left and even-numbered rows (wrong side rows—P all sts) from left to right.
BO.

 YARN A

 YARN B

 YARN C

 YARN D

YARN E

MIX-AND-MATCH

 17 155 210

89 Plain & Fancy

90 Diamonds

Special technique
Increasing and decreasing

NOTE At color changes, don't break off yarn, but carry color not in use up side of work.

Using yarn A, CO 3 sts and K 1 row.

Begin increase pattern.

ROW 1: (RS) K1, YO, K1, YO, K1.

ROW 2: Knit.

ROW 3: K1, YO, K to last st, YO, K1.

ROW 4: Knit.

Rep Rows 3 & 4 until there are 43 sts on needle, ending with a Row 4.

Join yarn B and begin decrease pattern.

NEXT ROW: Using yarn B, K2tog, K to last 2 sts, sl 1, K1, psso.

NEXT ROW: Using yarn B, K. Working alternate two-row stripes of yarn A and yarn B, rep 2-row dec patt until 3 sts rem on needle, ending with a Row 2.

NEXT ROW: K3tog.

Fasten off yarn.

MIX-AND-MATCH

 166 170 201

CO 34 sts.

ROW 1: (RS) K3, * P1, K8; rep from * to last 4 sts, P1, K3.

ROW 2: K1, P1, * K3, P6; rep from * to last 5 sts, K3, P1, K1.

ROW 3: K1, * P5, K4; rep from * to last 6 sts, P5, K1.

ROW 4: * K7, P2; rep from * to last 7 sts, K7.

ROW 5: K1, P to last st, K1.

ROW 6: Rep Row 4.

ROW 7: Rep Row 3.

ROW 8: K1, P1, * K3, P6; rep from * to last 5 sts, K3, P1, K1.

Rep Rows 1–8 five times more, ending with a Row 8.

Rep Row 1 once more.

BO.

MIX-AND-MATCH

 43 44 208

91 Light & Shade

 A B C D

92 Chain Gang

A B

ROWS 11 & 12: Using yarn B, K.

ROW 13: Using yarn A, K1, sl 1, * K6, sl 2; rep from * to last 8 sts, K6, sl 1, K1.

ROW 14: Using yarn A, K1, sl 1, * P6, sl 2; rep from * to last 8 sts, P6, sl 1, K1.

ROW 15: Using yarn B, rep Row 13.

ROW 16: Using yarn B, K.

Rep Rows 1–16 twice more, ending with a Row 16.

Rep Rows 1–10 once more.

BO.

Special technique
Working slip-stitch color patterns

NOTE Slip all stitches purlwise with yarn at wrong side of work. At color changes, don't break off yarn, but carry color not in use up side of work.

Using yarn A, CO 34 sts.

ROW 1: (RS) Using yarn A, K.

ROW 2: Using yarn A, K1, P to last st, K1.

ROWS 3 & 4: Using yarn B, K.

ROW 5: Using yarn A, K4, * sl 2, K6; rep from * to last 6 sts, sl 2, K4.

ROW 6: Using yarn A, K1, P3, * sl 2, P6; rep from * to last 6 sts, sl 2, P3, K1.

ROW 7: Using yarn B, rep Row 5.

ROW 8: Using yarn B, K.

ROWS 9 & 10: Using yarn A, rep Rows 1 & 2.

NOTE At color changes, don't break off yarn, but carry color not in use up side of work.

Using yarn A, CO 34 sts.

ROW 1: (RS) Using yarn A, K.

ROW 2: Using yarn A, K2, * P2, K2; rep from * to end.

ROWS 3 & 4: Using yarn A, rep Rows 1 & 2.

ROW 5: Using yarn B, K.

ROW 6: Using yarn B, K1, P1, * K2, P2; rep from * to last 4 sts, K2, P1, K1.

ROW 7: Using yarn B, rep Row 5.

ROW 8: Using yarn B, K1, P1, * K2, P2; rep from * to last 4 sts, K2, P1, K1.

Rep Rows 1–8 twice more, ending with a Row 8.

Break off yarns A & B; join yarns C & D.

Using yarn C instead of yarn A and yarn D instead of yarn B, rep Rows 1–8 three times more, ending with a Row 8.

NEXT ROW: Using yarn D, K.

BO.

MIX-AND-MATCH

13   136   178

MIX-AND-MATCH

34   70   89

93 Diamond Eyelets

Special technique
Working lace patterns

CO 33 sts and K 2 rows.
ROW 1: (RS) Knit.
ROW 2 AND EVERY ALT ROW: K1, P to last st, K1.
ROW 3: K4, * YO, sl 1, K1, psso, K6; rep from * to last 5 sts, YO, sl 1, K1, psso, K3.
ROW 5: K3, * YO, sl 1, K2tog, psso, YO, K5; rep from * to last 6 sts, YO, sl 1, K2tog, psso, YO, K3.
ROW 7: Rep Row 3.
ROW 9: Knit.
ROW 11: K8, * YO, sl 1, K1, psso, K6; rep from * to last st, K1.
ROW 13: K7, * YO, sl 1, K2tog, psso, YO, K5; rep from * to last 2 sts, K2.
ROW 15: Rep Row 11.
ROW 16: K1, P to last st, K1.
Rep Rows 1–16 once more, ending with a Row 16.
Rep Rows 1–10 once more.
BO.

MIX-AND-MATCH

94 Toronto

ROW 3: K13, sl 1, K2tog, psso, K13.
ROW 4: Knit.
ROW 5: K12, sl 1, K2tog, psso, K12.
ROW 6: Knit.
Break off yarn A; join yarn B.
Using yarn B, cont working in this way, dec 2 sts at the center of every RS (odd-numbered) row until 3 sts rem on needle, ending with a WS row.
NEXT ROW: K3tog.
Fasten off yarn.
Make one plain block in yarn A, one plain block in yarn B, one striped block in yarns A and B as above, and one striped block using yarn B instead of yarn A and yarn A instead of yarn B. Using the photograph as a guide to position, join the cast-on edges of the four blocks together using the overcast method of joining shown on page 122.

Special technique
Double decreasing

Plain block
CO 31 sts and K 1 row.
ROW 1: (RS) K14, sl 1, K2tog, psso, K14.
ROW 2: Knit.
ROW 3: K13, sl 1, K2tog, psso, K13.
ROW 4: Knit.
Cont working in this way, dec 2 sts at the center of every RS (odd-numbered) row until 3 sts rem on needle, ending with a WS row.
NEXT ROW: K3tog.
Fasten off yarn.

Striped block
Using yarn A, CO 31 sts and K 1 row.
ROW 1: (RS) K14, sl 1, K2tog, psso, K14.
ROW 2: Knit.

MIX-AND-MATCH

95 Classic Cables

ROWS 6 & 8: Rep Row 2.
ROWS 7 & 9: Rep Row 1.
ROW 10: * K6, P10; rep from * to last 6 sts, K6.
Rep Rows 1–10 three times more, ending with a Row 10.
Rep Rows 1–9. BO.

Special technique
Working cables

Special abbreviations
C10F = slip next 5 sts onto cable needle, hold at front of work, knit next 5 sts from left-hand needle, then knit stitches from cable needle.
C10B = slip next 5 sts onto cable needle, hold at back of work, knit next 5 sts from left-hand needle, then knit stitches from cable needle.

CO 38 sts.
ROW 1: (RS) K1, P5, K10, P6, K10, P5, K1.
ROW 2: * K6, P10; rep from * to last 6 sts, K6.
ROWS 3 & 4: Rep Rows 1 & 2.
ROW 5: K1, P5, C10F, P6, C10B, P5, K1.

MIX-AND-MATCH

 63   64   96

96 Button Up

Special technique
Increasing and decreasing

BUTTONS: 4 wooden buttons approximately ³/₄ in (18mm) in diameter

Special abbreviation
INC = increase by knitting into front and back of stitch.

Background block
Using yarn A, CO 33 sts.
ROWS 1–4: (RS) * K1, P1; rep from * to last st, K1.
ROW 5: [K1, P1] twice, K25, [P1, K1] twice.
ROW 6: [K1, P1] twice, P25, [P1, K1] twice.
Rep Rows 5 & 6 sixteen times more, ending with a Row 6.
Rep Rows 1–4 once more. BO.

Patch
Using yarn B, CO 2 sts.
Begin increase pattern.
ROW 1: (WS) Inc in first st, K1.
ROW 2: Inc in first st, K to end.
Rep 2-row inc patt until there are 22 sts on needle.
K one row.
Begin decrease pattern.
NEXT ROW: K2tog, K to end.
Cont in this way dec 1 st at beg of every row until 2 sts rem on needle.
NEXT ROW: K2tog.
Fasten off yarn.
After blocking, pin patch diagonally to center of background block. Position one button in each corner of patch and stitch in place through both layers.

MIX-AND-MATCH

 40   48   77

97 Little Flowers

Special technique
Working lace patterns

CO 33 sts.
ROW 1: (RS) Knit.
ROW 2 AND EVERY ALT ROW: K1, P to last st, K1.
ROW 3: Knit.
ROW 5: * K4, YO, sl 1, K1, psso; rep from * to last 3 sts, K3.
ROW 7: K2, * K2tog, YO, K1, YO, sl 1, K1, psso, K1; rep from * to last st, K1.
ROWS 9 & 11: Knit.
ROW 13: K1, YO, sl 1, K1, psso, * K4, YO, sl 1, K1, psso; rep from * to end.
ROW 15: K2, YO, sl 1, K1, psso, K1, K2tog, YO, * K1, YO, sl 1, K1, psso, K1, K2tog, YO; rep from * to last 2 sts, K2.
ROW 16: K1, P to last st, K1.
Rep Rows 1–16 once more, ending with a Row 16.
Rep Rows 1–12 once more.
BO.

MIX-AND-MATCH

 53 54 113

98 Scattered Leaves

ROW 15: K2tog tbl, K5, K2tog.
ROW 17: K2tog tbl, K3, K2tog.
ROW 19: K2tog tbl, K1, K2tog.
ROW 21: Sl 1, K2tog, psso.
Fasten off yarn, leaving a long yarn tail for stitching leaf to background.
Make one more leaf in yarn C and one more in yarn D.
After blocking, pin leaves to background block at random and stitch in place with matching yarn.

Special technique
Working lace patterns

Background block
Using yarn A, CO 33 sts.
ROW 1: (RS) Knit.
ROW 2: K1, P to last st, K1.
Rep Rows 1 & 2 twenty times more, ending with a Row 2.
BO.

Leaf motif
Using yarn B, CO 3 sts.
Work K1, P1, K1.
ROW 1: (RS) K1, YO, K1, YO, K1.
ROW 2 AND EVERY ALT ROW: K1, P to last st, K1.
ROW 3: K2, YO, K1, YO, K2.
ROW 5: K3, YO, K1, YO, K3.
ROW 7: K4, YO, K1, YO, K4.
ROW 9: K5, YO, K1, YO, K5.
ROW 11: K2tog tbl, K9, K2tog.
ROW 13: K2tog tbl, K7, K2tog.

MIX-AND-MATCH

 33 54 193

99 Softie

CO 37 sts.

ROW 1: (RS) K5, * P3, K5; rep from * to end.

ROW 2: P5, * K3, P5, rep from * to end.

ROWS 3 & 4: Rep Rows 1 & 2.

ROW 5: K1, P3, * K5, P3; rep from * to last st, K1.

ROW 6: P1, K3, * P5, K3; rep from * to last st, P1.

ROW 7: Rep Row 5.

ROW 8: P1, K3, * P5, K3; rep from * to last st, P1.

Rep Rows 1–8 four times more, ending with a Row 8.
Rep Rows 1–4 once more. BO.

MIX-AND-MATCH

100 Mosaic

Special technique
Working slip-stitch color patterns, working elongated stitches

NOTE Slip all stitches purlwise with yarn at wrong side of work. At color changes, don't break off yarn, but carry color not in use up side of work.

Using yarn A, CO 32 sts.

ROW 1: (WS) Using yarn A, K1, * K2, [P1 winding yarn twice around needle] twice, K2; rep from * to last st, K1.

ROW 2: Using yarn B, K1, * K2, [sl 1 dropping off yarn around needle of previous row] twice, K2; rep from * to last st, K1.

ROWS 3 & 4: Using yarn B, K1, * K2, sl 2, K2; rep from * to last st, K1.

ROW 5: Using yarn B, rep Row 3.

ROW 6: Using yarn B, rep Row 4.

ROW 7: Using yarn B, K1, * K2, [P1 winding yarn twice around needle] twice, K2; rep from * to last st, K1.

ROWS 8–12: Using yarn A, rep Rows 2–6.

ROW 13: Using yarn A, K1 * K2, [P1 winding yarn twice around needle] twice, K2; rep from * to last st, K1.

Rep Rows 2–13 four times more, ending with a Row 13.
Rep Rows 2–6 once more.
Rep Row 3 once more.

NEXT ROW: Using yarn A, K. BO.

MIX-AND-MATCH

101 Blue Seas

Special technique
Double decreasing

Using yarn A, CO 61 sts and K
1 row.
Row 1: (RS) K29, sl 1, K2tog, psso,
K29.
Row 2: Knit.
Row 3: K28, sl 1, K2tog, psso, K28.
Row 4: Knit.
Cont working in this way, dec 2 sts
at center of every RS (odd-
numbered) row, and changing
yarns in this color sequence:
Rows 5–10: Yarn A.
Rows 11–18: Yarn B.

Rows 19 & 20: Yarn A.
Rows 21 & 22: Yarn B.
Rows 23 & 24: Yarn C.
Rows 25 & 26: Yarn D.
Rows 27 & 28: Yarn A.
Rows 29 & 30: Yarn C.
Cont in yarn C only, until 3 sts rem
on needle, ending with a WS row.
Next Row: K3tog.
Fasten off yarn.

MIX-AND-MATCH

 3
 5
 105

OTHER COLOR SCHEMES

102 COLOR SCHEME: Two shades
of coral and a soft mauve are
combined in this block and
enhanced by a narrow stripe
in cream.

103 COLOR SCHEME: Areas in sage
green and rust show up well
against the main lemon and
yellow yarns and add a little extra
zing to the pattern.

104 COLOR SCHEME: Neutral
shades, surrounded by variegated
medium pink, make the perfect
block to combine for an afghan
for a baby girl.

102

103

104

Alternate Beads 105

OTHER COLOR SCHEMES

106   Ⓐ A Ⓑ

106 **COLOR SCHEME:** Crystal and silver beads add a beautiful, feminine sparkle to the coral background of this plain stockinette block.

107 **COLOR SCHEME:** Change the color balance of the original block by incorporating two different bead colors that provide an effective contrast with the background color.

108 **COLOR SCHEME:** Beads in pastel shades of pink and pale amethyst show up well against a neutral background.

107   Ⓐ Ⓐ B

108   Ⓐ A Ⓑ

Special technique
Applying beads with slip stitch

Special abbreviation
B = bead (bring yarn to front of work, slip next stitch, slide bead down yarn close to work, take yarn to back of work).

NOTE: Before casting on, thread beads onto yarn. If using two different colors of bead, follow this sequence: 6a, 5b, 6a, 5b, 6a, 5b, 6a. You will need 24 beads of color a and 15 of color b. Slip all stitches purlwise.

CO 33 sts.

Row 1: (RS) Knit.
Row 2 AND EVERY ALT ROW: Purl.
Row 3: K1, * B, K5; rep from * to last 2 sts, B, K1.
Rows 5 & 7: Knit.
Row 9: K4, * B, K5; rep from * to last 5 sts, B, K4.
Rows 11 & 13: Knit.
Row 15: Rep Row 3.
Rows 17 & 19: Knit.
Row 21: Rep Row 9.
Rows 23 & 25: Knit.

Row 27: Rep Row 3.
Rows 29 & 31: Knit.
Row 33: Rep Row 9.
Rows 35 & 37: Knit.
Row 39: Rep Row 3.
Row 40: Purl.
Row 41: Knit.
BO.

MIX-AND-MATCH

5

180

194

Bee Stitch Block

OTHER COLOR SCHEMES

110 **COLOR SCHEME:** Soft, neutral shades combine well in this block which would look good displayed against pine or other light wood furniture.

111 **COLOR SCHEME:** Warm shades of raspberry and lavender combine well and show off the textured stitch to great advantage.

112 **COLOR SCHEME:** Pale turquoise and lemon are a good color combination for a baby boy's afghan. For a girl, substitute mid and light shades of pink.

110   A B

111   A B

112   A B

Special technique
Working into the row below

Special abbreviation
K1B = knit one below (insert needle into stitch below next stitch on left-hand needle and knit it as usual, slipping the stitch above off the needle at the same time).

NOTE: At color changes, don't break off yarn, but carry color not in use up side of work.
Using yarn A, CO 27 sts and K 2 rows.

Join yarn B.
Row 1: (RS) Using yarn B, K1, * K1B, K1; rep from * to end.
Row 2: Using yarn B, K.
Row 3: Using yarn A, K2, K1B, * K1, K1B; rep from * to last 2 sts, K2.
Row 4: Using yarn A, K.
Rep Rows 1–4 twelve more times, ending with a Row 4.
NEXT ROW: Using yarn A, K.
BO.

MIX-AND-MATCH

20   **55**   **113**

Striped Basketweave `113`

✂ ⩳ A **B** C D E

OTHER COLOR SCHEMES

`114`

A B C D E

`115`

A B C D E

`116`

A B C D E

`114` **COLOR SCHEME:** Grays, naturals, and other neutral colors are perennial favorites for home furnishings and make a stylish afghan.

`115` **COLOR SCHEME:** Lavender and hot pinks work well together in this block while the single stripe of dark purple adds a welcome note of contrast.

`116` **COLOR SCHEME:** The lemon and green stripes combine well at the center of this striped block worked mainly in shades of turquoise.

Using yarn A, CO 36 sts.
Row 1: K4, * P4, K4; rep from * to end.
Row 2: P4, * K4, P4; rep from * to end.
Rows 3 & 4: Rep Rows 1 & 2.
Row 5: P4, * K4, P4; rep from * to end.
Row 6: K4, * P4, K4; rep from * to end.
Rows 7 & 8: Rep Rows 5 & 6.
Rep Rows 1–8 five times more, ending with a Row 8 and changing yarns in this color sequence: 8 rows in yarn B, 8 rows in yarn C, 8 rows in yarn D, 8 rows in yarn E, 8 rows in yarn A.
BO.

MIX-AND-MATCH

 `98`   `174`   `179`

117 Bobble Stripes

OTHER COLOR SCHEMES

118 **COLOR SCHEME:** Stripes in shades of pale and mid-toned greens provide contrast against a very dark background.

119 **COLOR SCHEME:** Cool colors such as turquoise and blue combine well with a soft, blue-toned pink and the result is very easy on the eye.

120 **COLOR SCHEME**: Unlike those used in the blocks 118 and 119, these warm, very vibrant colors offer a completely different effect.

118 A B C D

119 A B C D

120 A B C D

Special technique
Working bobbles

Special abbreviation
MB = make bobble ([K1, YO, K1, YO, K1] into next stitch, turn, K5, turn, P5, lift fourth, third, second, first stitch over fifth stitch and off needle).

Using yarn A, CO 37 sts.
Row 1: (RS) K1, P1, * K3, P2; rep from * to last 5 sts, K3, P1, K1.
Row 2: K2, * P3, K2; rep from * to end.

Row 3: K1, P1, * K1, MB, K1, P2, K3, P2; rep from * to last 7 sts, P2, K1, MB, K1, P1, K1.
Row 4: Rep Row 2.
Break off yarn A, join yarn B.
Row 5: Rep Row 1.
Row 6: Rep Row 2.
Row 7: K1, P1, * K3, P2, K1, MB, K1, P2; rep from * to last 5 sts, K3, P1, K1.
Row 8: Rep Row 2.
Break off yarn B, join yarn C, and rep Rows 1–4.
Break off yarn C, join yarn D, and rep Rows 5–8.

Break off yarn D, join yarn A, and rep Rows 1 & 2 eight more times, ending with a Row 2.
Join yarn B and rep Rows 1 & 2 six times, alternating 2 rows worked in yarn B with 2 rows worked in yarn A, and ending with a Row 2. BO.

MIX-AND-MATCH

 10   **48**   **137**

Crisscross `121`

OTHER COLOR SCHEMES

`122` **COLOR SCHEME:** Two contrasting shades of green show off the stylish geometric pattern of this block to full advantage.

`123` **COLOR SCHEME:** Many soft, pastel shades, such as turquoise and pink, look good when combined with each other or those of a similar tone.

`124` **COLOR SCHEME:** This color scheme, combined with the crisp, geometric pattern, makes a bold, modern statement.

122 **A** **B**

123 **A** **B**

124 **A** **B**

MIX-AND-MATCH

 39   **75**   **191**

Special technique
Double decreasing

Using yarn A, CO 31 sts and K 1 row.
Row 1: (RS) K14, sl 1, K2tog, psso, K14.
Row 2: Knit.
Row 3: K13, sl 1, K2tog, psso, K13.
Row 4: Knit.
Row 5: K12, sl 1, K2tog, psso, K12.
Row 6: Knit.
Break off yarn A, join yarn B.
Row 7: K11, sl 1, K2tog, psso, K11.

Row 8: K.
Using yarn B, cont working in this way, dec 2 sts at center of every RS (odd-numbered) row until 3 sts rem on the needle, ending with a WS row.
NEXT ROW: K3tog.
Fasten off yarn.
Make three more identical blocks. Using the photograph as a guide to position, join the cast-on edges of the four blocks together using the overcast method of joining shown on page 122.

Jacob's Ladder

OTHER COLOR SCHEMES

 COLOR SCHEME: With the main contrast now a variegated yarn, the block now looks totally different from the original.

 COLOR SCHEME: The rather masculine colors of this block would be perfect in a study, set against leather or tweed upholstery.

COLOR SCHEME: Two strong, clashing colors make each stripe stand out—this color scheme would make a cheerful throw for a child's bedroom.

126   A B

127   A B

128   A B

Special technique
Working slip-stitch color patterns

NOTE: Slip all stitches purlwise. At color changes, don't break off yarn, but carry color not in use up side of work.

Using yarn A, CO 35 sts and K 1 row.

Row 1: (RS) Using yarn B, K3, * wyib sl 1, K3; rep from * to end.

Row 2: Using yarn B, K3, * wyif sl 1, wyib K3; rep from * to end.

Row 3: Using yarn A, K1, * wyib sl 1, K3; rep from * to last 2 sts, wyib sl 1, K1.

Row 4: Using yarn A, K1, * wyif sl 1, wyib K3; rep from * to last 2 sts, wyif sl 1, wyib K1.

Rep Rows 1–4 seventeen times more, ending with a Row 4.

Using yarn A, K 2 rows.

BO.

MIX-AND-MATCH

 129   166   170

Purple Haze 129

OTHER COLOR SCHEMES

130

A B C D E

131

A B C D E

132

A B C D E

130 COLOR SCHEME: Soft corals combined with pale and medium turquoise make an unusual color scheme for a baby's room.

131 COLOR SCHEME: Neutral shades combine well in the color arrangement which shifts from warm camel to cool, pale gray.

132 COLOR SCHEME: Change the effect of the block by choosing hot, vibrant colors for the main stripes and contrast them with a strong, sunny yellow.

Special technique
Increasing and decreasing

Special abbreviation
inc = increase by knitting into front and back of stitch.

Using yarn A, CO 3 sts and K 1 row.
Begin increase pattern.
Row 1: (WS) Inc in first st, K to last st, inc in last st.
Row 2: Knit.
Rep 2-row inc patt until there are 21 sts on needle, ending with a

Row 1. Break off yarn A, join yarn B. Using yarn B, rep 2-row inc patt until there are 35 sts on needle, ending with a Row 1.
Break off yarn B, join yarn C. Using yarn C, rep 2-row inc patt until there are 43 sts on needle, ending with a Row 1.
Break off yarn C, join yarn D. Using yarn D, K 1 row.
Begin decrease pattern.
NEXT ROW: K2tog, K to last 2 sts, K2tog.
NEXT ROW: Knit.
Using yarn D, rep 2-row dec patt

until 35 sts rem on needle, ending with a Row 1.
Break off yarn D, join yarn E. Cont rep 2-row dec patt until 3 sts rem on needle, ending with a Row 2.
NEXT ROW: K3tog.
Fasten off yarn.

MIX-AND-MATCH

 69 **160** **166**

133 Beaded Diamond

 ● ○ x 13

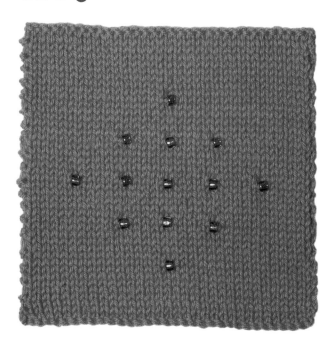

OTHER COLOR SCHEMES

134 **COLOR SCHEME:** For a stylish look, choose a neutral mocha for the background color and use pearl beads for contrast.

135 **COLOR SCHEME:** An afghan worked in shades of turquoise adorned with iridescent beads would look pretty in a Victorian-style room.

136 **COLOR SCHEME:** In contrast to the block above, a bold background color is enhanced with a sprinkling of silver beads.

134

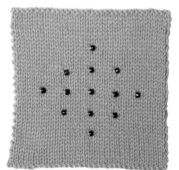
135

136

Special technique
Applying beads with slip stitch

Special abbreviation
B = bead (bring yarn to front of work, slip next stitch, slide bead down yarn, take yarn to back of work).

NOTE: Before casting on, thread 13 beads onto yarn. Slip all stitches purlwise.

CO 33 sts.

Row 1: (RS) Knit.

Row 2 AND EVERY ALT ROW: Purl.

Rows 3, 5 & 7: Knit.

Row 9: K16, B, K16.

Rows 11 & 13: Knit.

Row 15: K11, B, K4, B, K4, B, K11.

Rows 17 & 19: Knit.

Row 21: K6, B, K4, B, K4, B, K4, B, K4, B, K6.

Rows 23 & 25: Knit.

Row 27: Rep Row 15.

Rows 29 & 31: Knit.

Row 33: Rep Row 9.

Row 34: Purl.

Rows 35–40: Rep Rows 1 & 2.

Row 41: Knit.

BO.

MIX-AND-MATCH

 77 **117** **177**

Bricks 137

OTHER COLOR SCHEMES

138

 A B

139 A B

140 A B

138 **COLOR SCHEME:** Mocha and a soft, buttery cream offer a classic color combination which enhances the simple all-over pattern of this easy-to-knit block.

139 **COLOR SCHEME:** A warm shade of yellow framing a strong turquoise variegated yarn combine well for a bright, modern block.

140 **COLOR SCHEME:** African violet and deep mauve bring this simple pattern to life. This color scheme would enhance any setting.

MIX-AND-MATCH

 32
 78
 191

Special technique
Working slip-stitch color patterns

NOTE: Slip all stitches purlwise. At color changes, don't break off yarn, but carry color not in use up side of work.

Using yarn A, CO 35 sts.

Row 1: (RS) Using yarn A, K.

Row 2: Using yarn A, P.

Row 3: Using yarn B, K1, * sl 1, K3; rep from * to last 2 sts, sl 1, K1.

Row 4: Using yarn B, K1, * sl 1, P3; rep from * to last 2 sts, sl 1, K1.

Rows 5 & 6: Using yarn A, rep Rows 1 & 2.

Row 7: Using yarn B, K3, * sl 1, K3; rep from * to end.

Row 8: Using yarn B, K1, P2, * sl 1, P3; rep from * to last 4 sts, sl 1, P2, K1.

Rep Rows 1–8 four times more, ending with a Row 8.

Rep Rows 1–6 once more.

BO.

Random Bobbles

OTHER COLOR SCHEMES

142 **COLOR SCHEME:** Bobbles worked in a pale green yarn show up well against the very dark background of this block.

143 **COLOR SCHEME:** The use of variegated yarns enhances the texture provided by the randomly-placed bobbles.

144 **COLOR SCHEME:** With the choice of a light, rather than dark, background color, the block now looks totally different from the original.

142

143 A B

144

Special technique
Working contrast bobbles

Special abbreviation
MB = make bobble (using yarn B, [K1, P1, K1, P1, K1] into next stitch, turn, P5, turn, K5, turn, P2tog, P1, P2tog, turn, sl 1, K2tog, psso. Break off yarn B).

Using yarn A, CO 33 sts.
Row 1: (RS) Knit.
Row 2 AND EVERY ALT ROW: K1, P to last st, K1.

Row 3: Knit.
Row 5: K4, MB, K20, MB, K7.
Cont rep Rows 1 & 2, adding bobbles on the foll rows:
Row 13: K3, MB, K15, MB, K13.
Row 17: K15, MB, K17.
Row 19: K9, MB, K23.
Row 23: K27, MB, K5.
Row 29: K17, MB, K15.
Row 31: K8, MB, K24.
Row 37: K14, MB, K12, MB, K5.
Rows 38 & 40: Rep Row 2.
Rows 39 & 41: Rep Row 1.
BO.

MIX-AND-MATCH

 90   **140**   **166**

Corner Square 145

OTHER COLOR SCHEMES

146

Ⓐ Ⓑ Ⓒ Ⓓ

146 COLOR SCHEME: Contrasting shades of green in a strong pattern of stripes work well together in this easy-to-make block.

147 COLOR SCHEME: Soft, pretty, and very feminine, this color combination would produce a beautiful and unusual baby afghan.

148 COLOR SCHEME: The strong, deep red of the main color zings when enhanced by narrow stripes worked in very dark and very light colors.

147

Ⓐ Ⓑ Ⓒ Ⓓ

148

Ⓐ Ⓑ Ⓒ Ⓓ

MIX-AND-MATCH

92   125   141

Special technique
Double decreasing

NOTE: When introducing stripe color, don't break off yarn A. Instead, work two-row stripe in the required color, break off contrast yarn and continue to knit with yarn A.

Using yarn A, CO 61 sts and K 1 row.

Row 1: (RS) K29, sl 1, K2tog, psso, K29.

Row 2: Knit.

Row 3: K28, sl 1, K2tog, psso, K28.

Row 4: Knit.

Cont working in this way, dec 2 sts at center of every RS (odd-numbered) row and working 2-row stripes foll this color sequence:

Rows 5 & 6: Yarn B.

Rows 13 & 14: Yarn C.

Rows 21 & 22: Yarn D.

Rows 29 & 30: Yarn C.

Rows 37 & 38: Yarn B.

Cont in yarn A only, until 3 sts rem on needle, ending with a WS row.

NEXT ROW: K3tog. Fasten off yarn.

149 Fall Leaf

OTHER COLOR SCHEMES

150 **COLOR SCHEME:** Subtle shades of blue combine well with light and dark shades of lavender and purple.

151 **COLOR SCHEME:** Bright, clashing colors used in a striped pattern make a strong statement.

152 **COLOR SCHEME:** Neutral colors feature in this pretty leaf block. The ridged rows offer a change of texture.

Special abbreviation
M1 = make an extra stitch at beginning of row by working yarn over before knitting first stitch on needle.

Using yarn A, CO 3 sts.
Row 1: M1, K3.
Row 2: M1, K4.
Row 3: M1, K2, YO, K1, YO, K2.
Row 4: M1, K2, P3, K3.
Row 5: M1, K4, YO, K1, YO, K4.

MIX-AND-MATCH

Row 6: M1, K3, P5, K4.
Row 7: M1, K6, YO, K1, YO, K6.
Row 8: M1, K4, P7, K5.
Row 9: M1, K8, YO, K1, YO, K8.
Row 10: M1, K5, P9, K6.
Row 11: M1, K10, YO, K1, YO, K10.
Row 12: M1, K6, P11, K7.
Row 13: M1, K12, YO, K1, YO, K12.
Row 14: M1, K7, P13, K8.
Row 15: M1, K14, YO, K1, YO, K14.
Row 16: M1, K8, P15, K9.
Row 17: M1, K9, sl 1, K1, psso, K11, K2tog, K9.
Row 18: M1, K9, P13, K10.
Row 19: M1, K10, sl 1, K1, psso, K9, K2tog, K10.
Row 20: M1, K10, P11, K11.

Row 21: M1, K11, sl 1, K1, psso, K7, K2tog, K11.
Row 22: M1, K11, P9, K12.
Row 23: M1, K12, sl 1, K1, psso, K5, K2tog, K12.
Row 24: M1, K12, P7, K13.
Row 25: M1, K13, sl 1, K1, psso, K3, K2tog, K13.
Row 26: M1, K13, P5, K14.
Row 27: M1, K14, sl 1, K1, psso, K1, K2tog, K14.
Row 28: M1, K14, P3, K15.
Row 29: M1, K15, K3tog, K15.
Rows 30–33: M1, K to end.
Rows 34 & 37: M1, K1, P to last st, K1.
Rows 35 & 36: M1, K to end.

Row 38: M1, K to end. Break off yarn A, join yarn B.
Rows 39, 41 & 42: K2tog, K to end.
Rows 40 & 43: K2tog, P to end.
Row 44: K2tog, K to end. Break off yarn B, join yarn C, and rep Rows 39–44 once more.
Break off yarn C, join yarn D, and rep Rows 39–44 once more.
Break off yarn D, join yarn E, and rep Rows 39–44 once more.
Break off yarn E, join yarn B, and cont rep Rows 39 to 44 until 4 sts rem on needle.
NEXT ROW: K2tog twice. BO.

Speckled Bands 153

✂ ≣ Ⓐ B Ⓒ D Ⓔ Ⓕ

OTHER COLOR SCHEMES

154 **COLOR SCHEME:** Narrow, broken stripes of turquoise, larkspur, and putty look good against a soft, speckled blue background.

155 **COLOR SCHEME:** This color scheme uses three bright, strongly contrasting colors which show off the block's intricate stripe arrangement.

156 **COLOR SCHEME:** Delicately contrasting pastel shades are perfect against this textured camel background.

154 Ⓐ B Ⓒ D Ⓔ F

155 Ⓐ B Ⓒ D Ⓔ Ⓕ

156 Ⓐ B C Ⓓ Ⓔ F

Using yarn A, CO 33 sts.

Row 1: (RS) K1, * P1, K1; rep from * to end.

Rep Row 1, changing yarns foll this color sequence:

Rows 2–4: Yarn A.
Rows 5 & 6: Yarn B.
Rows 7–10: Yarn A.
Rows 11 & 12: Yarn C.
Rows 13–16: Yarn D.
Rows 17 & 18: Yarn E.
Rows 19 & 20: Yarn A.
Rows 21–24: Yarn F.
Rows 25 & 26: Yarn B.
Rows 27 & 28: Yarn F.

Rows 29 & 30: Yarn A.
Rows 31 & 32: Yarn F.
Rows 33–54: Yarn A.
BO.

MIX-AND-MATCH

 24 **65** **142**

Up and Over

OTHER COLOR SCHEMES

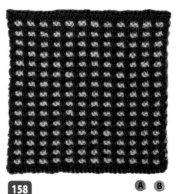

158 COLOR SCHEME: By simply reversing the light and dark tones of the main block, you can achieve a totally different effect.

159 COLOR SCHEME: Mix a marled yarn with a very dark solid color to create the perfect block for a masculine setting.

160 COLOR SCHEME: Fuchsia pink and lavender blend together to make the perfect color choice for a bed throw in a pretty, feminine bedroom.

158   A B

159   A B

160   A B

Special technique
Working slip-stitch color patterns

NOTE: Slip all stitches purlwise. At color changes, don't break off yarn, but carry color not in use up side of work.

Using yarn A, CO 39 sts.

Row 1: (RS) Using yarn A, K.

Row 2: Using yarn A, P.

Row 3: Using yarn B, K1, wyib sl 1, * K2, wyib sl 1; rep from * to last st, K1.

Row 4: Using yarn B, K1, wyif sl 1, * wyib K2, wyif sl 1; rep from * to last st, K1.

Rep Rows 1–4 fourteen times more, ending with a Row 4.

Using yarn A, rep Rows 1 & 2.

BO.

MIX-AND-MATCH

 26   85   106

Soft Stripes 161

✂ ⊒ Ⓐ Ⓑ Ⓒ Ⓓ

OTHER COLOR SCHEMES

162 Ⓐ Ⓑ Ⓒ Ⓓ

162 **COLOR SCHEME:** Change the effect of the block by using the darkest shade for the top stripe, graduating to the lightest shade for the bottom half.

163 **COLOR SCHEME:** Neutral shades of gray and camel are always a popular color choice but look even better when combined with a marled yarn.

164 **COLOR SCHEME:** A single stripe of hot fuchsia pink provides a strong contrast to the otherwise simple color scheme of three shades of mauve and blue.

163 Ⓐ Ⓑ Ⓒ Ⓓ

164 Ⓐ Ⓑ Ⓒ Ⓓ

Using yarn A, CO 33 sts.
Row 1: (RS) Knit.
Row 2: Purl.
Rows 3–20: Rep Rows 1 & 2, ending with a Row 2.
Row 21: Knit.
Break off yarn A, join yarn B.
Row 22: Purl.
Rows 23–28: Rep Rows 1 & 2, ending with a Row 2.
Break off yarn B, join yarn C.
Rows 29–34: Rep Rows 1 & 2, ending with a Row 2.
Row 35: Knit.
Break off yarn C, join yarn D.

Row 36: Purl.
Rows 37–42: Rep Rows 1 & 2, ending with a Row 2.
BO.

MIX-AND-MATCH

26   50   102

165 Four Square

OTHER COLOR SCHEMES

166 **COLOR SCHEME:** Mauve and lavender are highlighted with a variegated yarn—the perfect color choice for a bed throw in a pretty, fun, teenage bedroom.

167 **COLOR SCHEME:** An unusual color scheme of deep red, lavender, and lemon effectively displays the block's construction.

168 **COLOR SCHEME:** The warm yellows and oranges in this block would look good against natural pine or beech furniture.

166

167

168

Special technique
Double decreasing

Using yarn A, CO 31 sts and K 1 row.
Row 1: (RS) K14, sl 1, K2tog, psso, K14.
Row 2: Knit.
Row 3: K13, sl 1, K2tog, psso, K13.
Row 4: Knit.
Row 5: K12, sl 1, K2tog, psso, K12.
Row 6: Knit.
Cont working in this way, dec 2 sts at center of every RS (odd-numbered) row until 3 sts rem on the needle, ending with a WS row.

NEXT ROW: K3tog.
Fasten off yarn.
Make one block using yarn B, one using yarn C, and one using yarn D. Using the photograph as a guide to position, join the cast-on edges of the four blocks together using the overcast method of joining shown on page 122.

MIX-AND-MATCH

Furrows 169

OTHER COLOR SCHEMES

170

171

172

170 **COLOR SCHEME:** Solid and variegated shades of a single color blend the stripes together in a harmonious composition.

171 **COLOR SCHEME:** Rich, deep shades of red are very masculine colors—ideal for a throw displayed against leather or dark wood furniture.

172 **COLOR SCHEME:** The textured, striped surface of this block is brought to life with glowing orange and bright yellow.

NOTE: At color changes, don't break off yarn, but carry color not in use up side of work.

Using yarn A, CO 33 sts.

Row 1: (WS) Knit.

Join yarn B.

Row 2: K1, P to last st, K1.

Row 3: Knit.

Rep Rows 1–3 fourteen times more, at the same time change yarn color every 2 rows.

BO.

MIX-AND-MATCH

 136

145

 178

173 Waffle Stripes

OTHER COLOR SCHEMES

174 COLOR SCHEME: A vivid visual statement is created with hot, vibrant shades of raspberry pink and deep mauve.

175 COLOR SCHEME: This is such a pretty block to use for making a baby girl's afghan. The deep red strips are softened by the variegated pink yarn.

176 COLOR SCHEME: The contrast of pale blue stripes against a darker blue background offers a much softer appearance.

174   A B

175 A B

176   A B

NOTE: At color changes, don't break off yarn, but carry color not in use loosely up side of work.

Using yarn A, CO 34 sts.

Row 1: (RS) K1, * K2, P1; rep from * to last 3 sts, K3.

Row 2: K1, * P2, K1; rep from * to end.

Row 3: Rep Row 1.

Row 4: Knit.

Join yarn B.

Rows 5–8: Using yarn B, rep Rows 1–4.

Rep Rows 1–8 five times more, ending with a Row 8.

BO.

MIX-AND-MATCH

63 133 205

Patch 177

OTHER COLOR SCHEMES

178 **COLOR SCHEME:** Bright pink stitching brings shades of mauve to life. The stitches themselves provide a strong contrast with the stockinette stitch background.

179 **COLOR SCHEME:** This cheerful color scheme combines a cherry red patch with a pale pink variegated background, enhanced by burgundy stitches.

180 **COLOR SCHEME:** Change the tonal balance of the original block by using a light color to work the background and a darker shade for the patch.

178   A B C

179   A B C

180   A B C

MIX-AND-MATCH

 31   **163**   **182**

Special techniques
Working color patterns by the intarsia method; embroidering on knitting

Using yarn A, CO 33 sts.
Row 1: (RS) Knit.
Row 2: Purl.
Rep Rows 1 & 2 eleven times more.
Row 25: K19 in yarn A, join yarn B and K14 in yarn B.
Row 26: P14 in yarn B, P19 in yarn A.
Row 27: K19 in yarn A, K14 in yarn B.

Rep Rows 26 & 27 seven times more, ending with a Row 27.
NEXT ROW: Rep Row 26.
BO.
Using a length of yarn C threaded in a tapestry needle, make evenly spaced straight stitches at right angles to the edges of the patch where they join the main part of the block.

Solid Leaf

Row 15: M1, K7, YO, K13, YO, K7.

Row 16: M1, K7, P15, K8.

Row 17: M1, K to end.

Row 18: M1, K8, P15, K9.

Row 19: M1, K9, sl 1, K1, psso, K11, K2tog, K9.

Row 20: M1, K9, P13, K10.

Row 21: M1, K10, sl 1, K1, psso, K9, K2tog, K10.

Row 22: M1, K10, P11, K11.

Row 23: M1, K11, sl 1, K1, psso, K7, K2tog, K11.

Row 24: M1, K11, P9, K12.

Row 25: M1, K12, sl 1, K1, psso, K5, K2tog, K12.

Row 26: M1, K12, P7, K13.

Row 27: M1, K13, sl 1, K1, psso, K3, K2tog, K13.

Row 28: M1, K13, P5, K14.

Row 29: M1, K14, sl 1, K1, psso, K1, K2tog, K14.

Row 30: M1, K14, P3, K15.

Row 31: M1, K15, sl 1, K2tog, psso, K15.

Rows 32–39: M1, K to end.

Rows 40 & 41: K to end.

Join yarn B.

Cont in patt as folls, changing yarn color every 2 rows to end.

Row 42: P2tog, P to end.

Rows 43 & 44: K2tog, K to end.

Row 45: P2tog, P to end.

Rep Rows 43–45 until 2 sts rem on needle.

BO.

Special abbreviation

M1 = make an extra stitch at beginning of row by working yarn over in front before knitting first stitch on needle.

NOTE: When working color changes in striped section of block, don't break off yarn, but carry color not in use up side of work.

MIX-AND-MATCH

Using yarn A, CO 1 st.

Row 1: M1, K1.

Row 2: M1, K2.

Row 3: M1, K1, YO, K1, YO, K1.

Row 4: M1, K1, P3, K2.

Row 5: M1, K2, YO, K3, YO, K2.

Row 6: M1, K2, P5, K3.

Row 7: M1, K3, YO, K5, YO, K3.

Row 8: M1, K3, P7, K4.

Row 9: M1, K4, YO, K7, YO, K4.

Row 10: M1, K4, P9, K5.

Row 11: M1, K5, YO, K9, YO, K5.

Row 12: M1, K5, P11, K6.

Row 13: M1, K6, YO, K11, YO, K6.

Row 14: M1, K6, P13, K7.

OTHER COLOR SCHEMES

182 COLOR SCHEME: Green and brown is very masculine color scheme—perfect against leather-covered furniture.

183 COLOR SCHEME: These soft colors would be perfect for a small, strongly patterned afghan for a baby boy.

184 COLOR SCHEME: Claret and a two-toned marled yarn in shades of gray combine beautifully.

Counterpoint 185

OTHER COLOR SCHEMES

186

186 COLOR SCHEME: Art Deco colors of hot orange and bright lime green work well with this unusual geometric pattern.

187 COLOR SCHEME: Cool pastel shades look great together, particularly this clear, pale green, light blue, and soft mauve.

188 COLOR SCHEME: The two-toned marled yarn used in this block adds interest to the plain areas of strong red and blue.

 187

188

MIX-AND-MATCH

131   152   163

A B C

Special technique
Double decreasing

Using yarn A, CO 31 sts and K 1 row.
Row 1: (RS) K14, sl 1, K2tog, psso, K14.
Row 2: Knit.
Row 3: K13, sl 1, K2tog, psso, K13.
Row 4: Knit.
Cont working in this way, dec 2 sts at center of every RS (odd-numbered) row, and working rows in contrast yarn following this color sequence:

Rows 5–14: Yarn B.
Rows 15–28: Yarn C.
NEXT ROW: K3tog.
Fasten off yarn.
Make one identical block.
Make two more blocks using yarn B instead of yarn A, yarn C instead of yarn B, and yarn A instead of yarn B.
Using the photograph as a guide to position, join the four blocks together using the overcast method of joining shown on page 122.

189 Oblique Stripe

 A B C

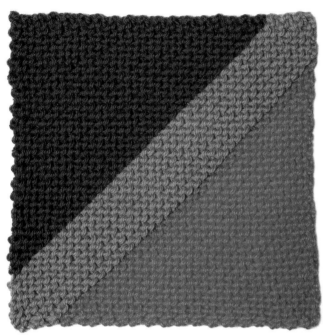

OTHER COLOR SCHEMES

190 **COLOR SCHEME:** A soft, warm cocoa brown combines well with light and medium shades of blue to work this boldly patterned block.

191 **COLOR SCHEME:** A bold slash of burnt orange across the block adds life to a neutral color scheme of medium gray and oatmeal.

192 **COLOR SCHEME:** Two shades of green plus lemon are used here in a gradation from dark to light.

190 A B C

191 A B C

192 A B C

Special technique
Increasing and decreasing

Special abbreviation
inc = increase by knitting into front and back of stitch.

Using yarn A, CO 3 sts and K 1 row.
Begin increase pattern.
Row 1: (WS) Inc in first st, K to last st, inc in last st.
Row 2: Knit.
Rep 2-row inc patt until there are 37 sts on needle, ending with a Row 1.

Break off yarn A, join yarn B. Using yarn B, rep 2-row patt until there are 43 sts on needle, ending with a Row 2.
Begin decrease pattern.
Next Row: K2tog, K to last 2 sts, K2tog.
Next Row: Knit.
Rep 2-row patt until 37 sts rem on needle, ending with a Row 1.
Break off yarn B, join in yarn C.
Cont rep 2-row dec patt until 3 sts rem on the needle, ending with a Row 2.
Next Row: K3tog. Fasten off yarn.

MIX-AND-MATCH

 18   **87**   **151**

Ridges 193

OTHER COLOR SCHEMES

194

A B

194 COLOR SCHEME: Blue is a popular color choice for bedroom decorations and this combination would make a lovely, textured throw to cover a wicker chair.

195 COLOR SCHEME: Classic brown and cream shades combine well in this block which would look good displayed against pine or other light wood furniture.

196 COLOR SCHEME: Lime green, a bright shade of yellow green, is exciting beside ridged stripes in zinging orange.

195

A B

196

A B

NOTE: At color changes, don't break off yarn, but carry color not in use up side of work.

Using yarn A, CO 33 sts.

Row 1: (RS) Using yarn A, K.

Row 2: Using yarn A, P.

Join yarn B.

Row 3: Using yarn B, K.

Row 4: Using yarn B, K.

Rep Rows 1–4 twelve times more, ending with a Row 4.

Using yarn A, rep Rows 1 & 2.

BO.

MIX-AND-MATCH

 19 52 104

Harris

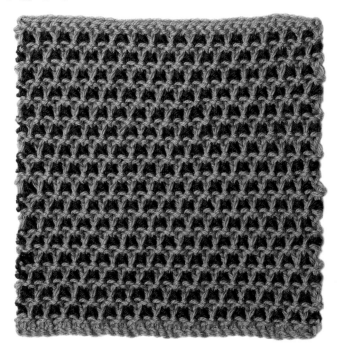

OTHER COLOR SCHEMES

 COLOR SCHEME: A dark shade of blue frames variegated green and brown making a strong, masculine statement.

 COLOR SCHEME: Enhance the stitch pattern by contrasting hot fuchsia pink with clear, mid-toned lavender.

COLOR SCHEME: Mushroom shows up well against soft white, a versatile tint which looks as good with bright colors as with neutral shades.

198 Ⓐ Ⓑ

199 Ⓐ Ⓑ

200 Ⓐ Ⓑ

Special technique
Working slip-stitch color patterns

NOTE: Slip all stitches knitwise. At color changes, don't break off yarn, but carry color not in use up side of work.

Using yarn A, CO 33 sts.

Row 1: (RS) Using yarn A, K.

Row 2: Knit.

Row 3: Using yarn B, * K1, sl 1; rep from * to last st, K1.

Row 4: Using yarn B, * K1, yf, sl 1, yb; rep from * to last st, K1.

Rows 5 & 6: Using yarn A, K.

Row 7: Using yarn B, * sl 1, K1; rep from * to last st, sl 1.

Row 8: Using yarn B, * sl 1, yb, K1, yf; rep from * to last st, sl 1.

Rep Rows 1–8 seven times more, ending with a Row 8.

Using yarn A, K 2 rows.

BO.

MIX-AND-MATCH

 70
 145
 212

V-stripes 201

OTHER COLOR SCHEMES

202 A B

203 A B

204 A B

202 **COLOR SCHEME:** An unusual combination of dark blue and a variegated yarn.

203 **COLOR SCHEME:** A brighter, livelier combination of one solid and one variegated yarn.

204 **COLOR SCHEME:** Mushroom and hop green would be a good choice in a sunny garden room.

MIX-AND-MATCH

 84   **129**   **166**

Special technique
Working slip-stitch color patterns

Special abbreviation
pwyt = purl next stitch winding yarn twice around needle.

NOTE: Slip all stitches purlwise. At color changes, don't break off yarn, but carry color not in use loosely up side of work.
Using yarn A, CO 33 sts.
Row 1: (RS) Using yarn A, K.
Row 2: Using yarn A, P1, * pwyt, P5; rep from * to last 2 sts, pwyt, P1.
Row 3: Using yarn B, K1, * wyib sl 1 dropping extra loop, K5; rep from * to last 2 sts, wyib sl 1 dropping extra loop, K1.
Row 4: Using yarn B, P1, * wyif sl 1, P5; rep from * to last 2 sts, wyif sl 1, P1.
Row 5: Using yarn B, K1, * wyib sl 1, K5; rep from * to last 2 sts, wyib sl 1, K1.
Row 6: Using yarn B, P4, * pwyt, P5; rep from * to last 5 sts, pwyt, P4.
Row 7: Using yarn A, K4, * wyib sl 1 dropping extra loop, K5; rep from * to last 5 sts, wyib sl 1 dropping extra loop, K4.
Row 8: Using yarn A, P4, * wyif sl 1, P5; rep from * to last 5 sts, wyif sl 1, P4.
Row 9: Using yarn A, K4, * wyib sl 1, K5; rep from * to last 5 sts, wyib sl 1, K4.
Row 10: Using yarn A, P1, * pwyt, P5; rep from * to last 2 sts, pwyt, P1.
Rep Rows 3–10 four times more.
Rep Rows 3–5 once more.
NEXT ROW: Using yarn B, P. BO.

205 Big Cross

OTHER COLOR SCHEMES

206 **COLOR SCHEME:** Two strongly contrasting shades of pink show off the bold cross pattern of this four-part block beautifully.

207 **COLOR SCHEME:** An afghan worked in bright, cheerful colors, such as yellow and turquoise, will add life and warmth to any neutral decorating scheme.

208 **COLOR SCHEME:** Medium turquoise and lavender, two cool colors with a similar tonal balance, completely alter the appearance of the block.

206   Ⓐ B

207   Ⓐ B

208   Ⓐ B

Special technique
Double decreasing

Using yarn A, CO 31 sts and K 1 row.

Row 1: (RS) K14, sl 1, K2tog, psso, K14.

Row 2: Knit.

Row 3: K13, sl 1, K2tog, psso, K13.

Row 4: Knit.

Row 5: K12, sl 1, K2tog, psso, K12.

Row 6: K1, P23, K1.

Row 7: K11, sl 1, K2tog, psso, K11.

Row 8: Knit.

Row 9: K10, sl 1, K2tog, psso, K10.

Cont working in this way, dec 2 sts at center of every RS (odd-numbered) row until 17 sts rem on needle, ending with a RS row. Break off yarn A, join yarn B.

Row 14: Using yarn B, K.

Row 15: K7, sl 1, K2tog, psso, K7.

Row 16: Knit.

Cont working in this way until 3 sts rem on needle, ending with a WS row.

NEXT ROW: K3tog.

Fasten off yarn.

Make three more identical blocks.

Using the photograph as a guide to position, join the cast-on edges of the four blocks together using the overcast method of joining shown on page 122.

MIX-AND-MATCH

Little Waves 209

⚹ ⚹ ≋ Ⓐ Ⓑ Ⓒ D

OTHER COLOR SCHEMES

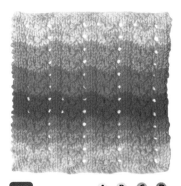

210   Ⓐ Ⓑ Ⓒ Ⓓ

210 COLOR SCHEME: The addition of some hot, deep pinks brings warmth to the pastel pinks and white.

211 COLOR SCHEME: A sunny shade of yellow contrasts well with these cool blues.

212 COLOR SCHEME: This subtle, rather sophisticated color scheme in shades of purple will enhance the natural beauty of wood and terracotta.

211   Ⓐ Ⓑ Ⓒ Ⓓ

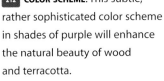

MIX-AND-MATCH

95 127 133

212   Ⓐ Ⓑ Ⓒ Ⓓ

Special technique
Working yarn overs

NOTE: When working a YO between a K st and a P st, wrap the yarn around the needle and then bring forward. When working a YO between a P st and a K st, leave the yarn forward and knit.

Using yarn A, CO 32 sts.
Row 1: Knit.
Row 2: Purl.
Row 3: K3, * YO, P1, P3tog, P1, YO, K2; rep from * to last st, K1.
Row 4: Purl.
Rep Rows 1–4 eleven times more, ending with a Row 4 and changing yarns in this color sequence: 4 more rows in yarn A (8 rows total), 4 rows in yarn B, 4 rows in yarn C, 8 rows in yarn D, 8 rows in yarn C, 8 rows in yarn B, 8 rows in yarn A.
NEXT ROW: Using yarn A, K.
BO.

Techniques

In this chapter, you'll find a refresher course to help you make and join the blocks shown in the directory, including tips on working lace, cable, and multicolored patterns. There are also instructions for making a variety of stylish edgings and details of the actual yarns used to work the blocks.

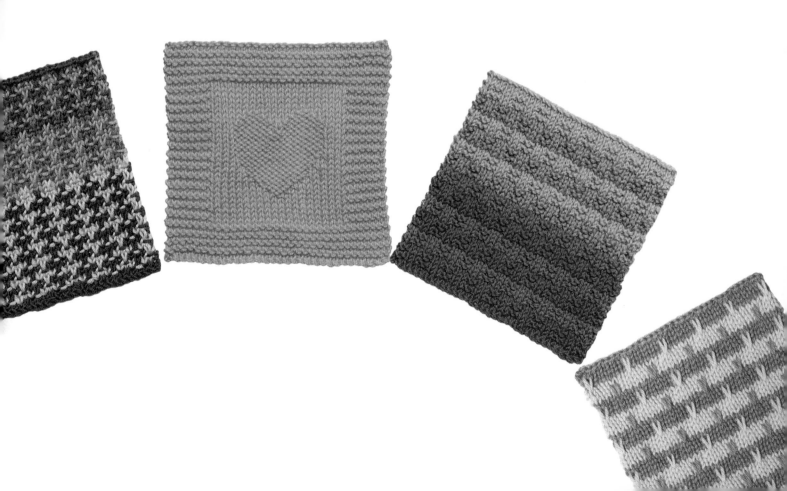

Yarn choices

Each block in the book can be knitted with your own choice of yarn. As well as selecting colors (see pages 14 and 15), you also have to decide on fiber composition. The author prefers pure wool yarns and has used a smooth, double-knitting-weight yarn to make the blocks; but there are times when synthetic yarns are preferable, particularly for babies' items, which require frequent washing. You might decide to use a pure cotton or blended acrylic/cotton yarn, or to be adventurous and incorporate some textured yarns such as mohair, tweed, or ribbon yarn.

The swatches show block 74, Alternate Eyelets (see page 66), worked in three different yarn weights. By using different yarns, the appearance of the block changes considerably, from light and lacy to thick and chunky.

Calculating yarn amounts

The most reliable way to work out how much yarn you need is to buy a ball of yarn in each color required for the project, and knit some sample swatches. The amount of yarn per ball or skein can vary slightly between different colors of the same yarn because of the dyes used, so it's a good idea to make the samples using the actual colors you intend to knit.

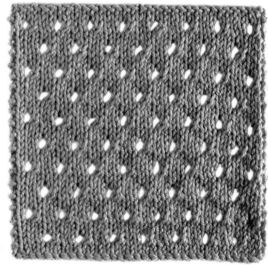

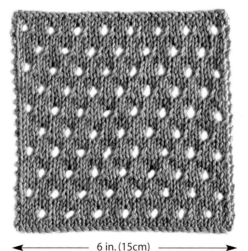

←——— 5 in. (13cm) ———→   ←——— 6 in. (15cm) ———→   ←——— 7 in. (18cm) ———→

SWATCH 1 is knit in 4-ply Soft 100% Merino Wool from Rowan, using size 3 (3.25mm) Bryspun needles. After blocking, the swatch measures 5 in. (13cm) across. The light, softly twisted yarn creates a delightfully lacy block.

SWATCH 2 is knit in Matchmaker Double Knitting 100% Merino Wool from Jaeger, which is the same weight as the yarns used to make all the blocks in the directory. Worked with size 6 (4mm) Bryspun needles, the swatch measures 6 in. (15cm) across after blocking.

SWATCH 3 is knit in Matchmaker Aran 100% Merino Wool from Jaeger with size 7 (4.5mm) Bryspun needles. After blocking, it measures 7 in. (18cm) across. The pretty lace stitch is less successful worked in such a heavy yarn and loses its light, delicate appeal.

Knitting a sample swatch

Using a suitable needle size (see below for a yarn/needle compatibility chart), work three blocks in each pattern you intend to use, making sure that you allow at least 3 in. (8cm) of spare yarn at every color change. This will compensate for the extra yarn you'll need when weaving in the ends.

Unravel the three finished blocks and carefully measure the amount of yarn used for each color in each block. Take the average yardage and multiply it by the number of blocks you intend to make. Don't forget to add extra yarn to your calculations for joining the blocks together and for knitting any edgings.

Needles

The basic knitting tool is a pair of needles. Single-pointed, straight knitting needles come in a range of sizes from small (US size 0 / 2mm) to large (US size 19 / 15mm) to suit different weights of yarn. Straight needles are made from aluminum, wood, bamboo, or different types of plastic. They are usually available in two lengths: 10 in. (25cm) and 14 in. (36cm). Choose whichever type of needle feels best in your hands and is comfortable to use.

Useful yarn/needle combinations

Sport weight (4-ply)	US sizes 2–4 (2.5–3.5mm)
Double knitting (DK)	US sizes 4–7 (3.5–4.5mm)
Worsted weight (Aran)	US sizes 7–9 (4.5–5.5mm)

Abbreviations

This list includes common knitting abbreviations. Any special abbreviations are shown with the relevant patterns.

alt	alternate
BO	bind off
CO	cast on
cont	continue
dec	decrease/ decreasing
foll	following
inc	increase/ increasing
K	knit
K2tog	knit two stitches together
P	purl
P2tog	purl two stitches together
psso	pass slipped stitch over
p2sso	pass two slipped stitches over
rem	remain/ remainder/ remaining
rep	repeat
RS	right side of work
sl	slip next stitch
tbl	through back loops
tog	together
WS	wrong side of work
wyib	with yarn at back of work
wyif	with yarn in front of work
YO	yarn over needle to make extra stitch

How to start

Knitting techniques are based on two simple stitches: the knit stitch and the purl stitch. Once you get the hang of casting on, working the basic stitches, and binding off, it's easy to move on to the more complex techniques including cables and multicolored patterns. There is no right and wrong way to hold yarn and needles; choose the way that feels the most natural and comfortable to you.

Making a slip knot

The first step in knitting is casting on—creating the required number of stitches on one needle. First, you need to make a slip knot in the yarn about 6 in. (15cm) away from the end of the yarn, and put the loop of the knot onto a needle.

1 Coil the yarn into a loop, as shown, then insert the needle underneath the bottom strand and bring it forward.

2 Gently pull one end of the yarn to tighten the knot, then pull the other end of the yarn to bring the knot close to the needle.

Casting on

This method of casting on, the cable cast-on, makes a neat, strong edge. If you find that your cast-on edge is too tight and pulls across the lower edge of the block, simply substitute a larger sized left needle.

1 Hold the needle with the slip knot in your left hand, and the other needle in your right hand. Insert the tip of the right needle into the front of the slip loop, take the yarn around the right needle and pull a stitch through. Transfer the stitch to the left needle.

2 From this point, insert the right needle between the stitches, take the yarn around the needle and pull a stitch through each time. Transfer each new stitch onto the left needle as in step 1. Repeat until you have cast on the required number of stitches.

Working the basic stitches

There are two basic stitches in knitting—the knit stitch and the purl stitch. To make a row of stitches, work into each stitch on the left needle until they have all been transferred to the right needle. Then move the needle with the stitches to your left hand to work the next row.

Making a knit stitch

This is the first stitch to master. If every stitch of every row is a knit stitch, the result is called garter stitch and it looks exactly the same on both sides of the work. Practice working knit stitches as follows.

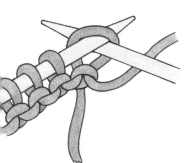

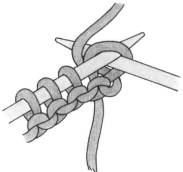

1 Hold the needle with the cast-on stitches in your left hand. With the yarn behind the needle, insert the tip of the right needle into the front of the first stitch from left to right as shown.

2 Holding the yarn in your right hand, take it behind both needles, then bring it up and around the tip of the right needle.

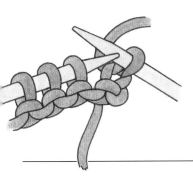

3 Using the right needle, pull a loop of yarn through the stitch to make a new stitch on the right needle. Slip the old stitch off the left needle. Repeat along the row.

Making a purl stitch

Purl stitches are the opposite of knit stitches. The best-known combination of knit and purl stitches is called stockinette stitch, which is made by knitting and purling alternate rows. Knit rows form the smooth right side of stockinette stitch and the purl rows form the ridged wrong side.

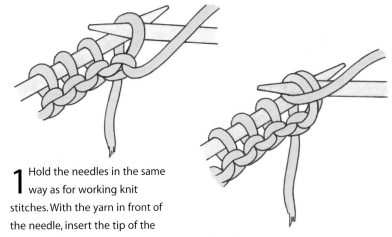

1 Hold the needles in the same way as for working knit stitches. With the yarn in front of the needle, insert the tip of the right needle into the front of the first stitch from right to left.

2 Holding the yarn in your right hand, loop it around the tip of the right needle.

3 Use the tip of the right needle to draw a loop of yarn through to make a new stitch on the right needle. Slip the old stitch off the left needle. Repeat along the row.

Joining new yarn

When you come to the end of a ball of yarn, or when you need to change the yarn color in a pattern, always do this at the beginning or end of a row to avoid unsightly joins in the middle of your knitting.

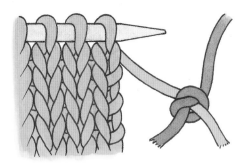

Tie the end of the new yarn loosely around the old yarn, leaving a tail of about 6 in. (15cm). Gently tighten the knot and slip it up the old yarn until it rests against the needle. Untie the knot later and darn the ends into the edge of the knitting.

Binding off

When your knitting has reached the correct length, you need to finish off the last row of stitches to prevent them from unraveling. This is called binding off. (If your bound-off edge is too tight, a larger sized right needle should be substituted.)

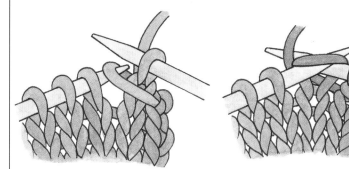

1 Knit the first two stitches in the usual way. Insert the tip of the left needle into the first stitch on the right needle, and lift it over the second stitch and off the right needle.

2 One stitch now remains on the right needle. Knit the next stitch on the left needle, insert the left needle into the first stitch on the right needle and repeat as in step 1. Repeat along the row, cut the yarn leaving a tail of about 6 in. (15cm), and pull the tail through the stitch remaining on the right needle.

Gauge

All the blocks in the book measure 6 in. (15cm) across after blocking. As no two people will knit to exactly the same gauge, even when working with identical needles and yarn, you should make a sample block using the recommended weight of yarn (DK) and the specified size of needles. Measure the block. It should be slightly smaller than 6 in. (15cm) across so that when blocked it will measure exactly 6 in. (15cm) square.

As a general rule, if your block turns out to be smaller than required, make another sample using needles one size larger. (Also do this when the knit fabric feels tight and hard.) If your block is larger than required, make another sample using needles one size smaller. (Also do this if the knit fabric feels loose and floppy.) Gauge can also be affected by the fiber composition of yarn and the size and brand of needles, so you may need to make several blocks using different needle sizes until you're happy with the size and feel of your block.

Working stitch patterns

Stitch patterns are worked using combinations of the basic knit and purl stitches. For some patterns, knit and purl stitches are worked as already described; for other patterns, the stitches are manipulated in various ways. For example, the needle may be inserted in a different direction, stitches may be slipped from needle to needle without being worked, or the number of stitches on the needle may be increased or decreased.

Working into the back of stitches

The front of each stitch is always the loop closest to you, whether working right-side rows or wrong-side rows. Unless stated in the pattern instructions, always work into the front loop of the stitch. When instructed to work into the back loop, work knit and purl stitches as shown here.

1 To knit into the back loop of a stitch, insert the tip of the right needle under the left needle and into the loop of the stitch farthest from you, and knit this loop in the usual way.

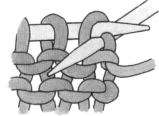

2 To purl into the back loop of a stitch, insert the tip of the right needle from back to front into the loop farthest from you, and purl this loop in the usual way.

Slipping stitches

Many patterns tell you to slip one or more stitches. This is done by passing the stitches from the left needle to the right needle without actually working them. Unless instructed otherwise, slip all slipped stitches knitwise.

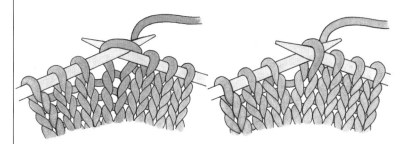

1 To slip a stitch knitwise, insert the tip of the right needle into the next stitch on the left needle, as if you were knitting the stitch. Pull this stitch off the left needle. The stitch is now on the right needle.

2 To slip a stitch purlwise, insert the tip of the right needle into the next stitch on the left needle, as if you were purling the stitch. Pull this stitch off the left needle. The stitch is now on the right needle.

Knitting into the row below

Found in both rib and colorwork patterns, this technique makes a soft, thick fabric. Instead of making a knit stitch out of the next stitch on the left needle, the right needle is inserted into the previous row.

1 Insert the tip of the right needle (from front to back) into the center of the stitch on the row directly below the next stitch on the left needle. Knit the stitch as usual, slipping the top stitch off the left needle without working it.

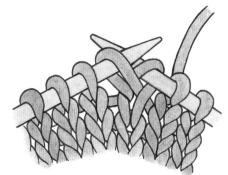

Working increases and decreases

Increases and decreases alter the number of stitches on the needle in any given row. They are used when knitting lace patterns and also when working block patterns diagonally from corner to corner.

Working a bar increase

A bar increase is often worked on the knit side of the work. It is an easy increase made by knitting twice (or by purling twice) into the same stitch.

1 Insert the tip of the right needle into the stitch to be increased, as if you were going to knit it. Take the yarn around the needle and knit the stitch but do not slip it off the left needle.

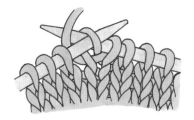

2 Insert the right needle into the back of the same stitch, take the yarn around the needle and pull it through to make a second stitch. Slip the original stitch off the left needle.

Working a make one increase

This increase is less visible than a bar increase. One extra stitch is worked into the horizontal strand of yarn between two ordinary stitches. Knit through the back loop of the lifted strand to prevent a small hole forming.

1 Insert the tip of the right needle (from front to back) into the strand between the last stitch worked and the first stitch on the left needle. Place it on the left needle.

2 Knit this strand through the back loop and slip the loop off the left needle to leave a new stitch on the right needle.

Working two stitches together

The simplest way of decreasing one stitch at a time is to knit or purl two stitches together. Usually, the knit version is used on right-side rows and the purl version on wrong-side rows.

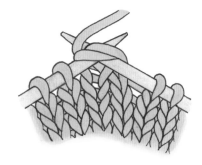

1 To knit two stitches together, insert the right needle (from front to back) into the next two stitches on the left needle, as if you were going to knit. Take the yarn around the needle and pull through to decrease one stitch.

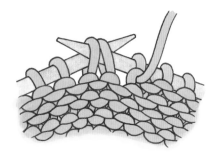

2 To purl two stitches together, insert the right needle into the front loops of the next two stitches on the left needle, as if you were going to purl. Take the yarn around the needle and pull through to decrease one stitch.

Working a single decrease

This method of decreasing one stitch at a time is usually worked on the right side of the work. Take care to slip stitches knitwise to prevent the stitches becoming twisted.

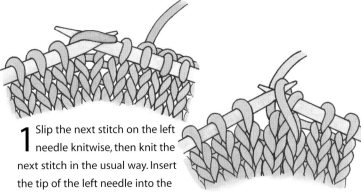

1 Slip the next stitch on the left needle knitwise, then knit the next stitch in the usual way. Insert the tip of the left needle into the front of the slipped stitch.

2 Lift the slipped stitch over the knit stitch and off the right needle. One stitch has now been decreased.

Working a double decrease

This method of decreasing reduces the stitches by two at a time. It is worked in a similar way to the single decrease, but two stitches are knitted together before the slipped stitch is passed over.

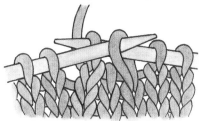

1 Slip the next stitch on the left needle knitwise, then knit the next two stitches together to decrease one stitch. Insert the tip of the left needle into the front of the slipped stitch. Lift the slipped stitch over the decreased stitches and off the right needle to decrease a second stitch. Two stitches have now been decreased.

Working basic cables

A basic cable can be worked over a group of four, six, or more stitches, twisting to either the left or right. A six-stitch cable is illustrated here. It is being worked to the front (which twists the stitches to the left and is abbreviated as C6F) and to the back (which twists the stitches to the right and is abbreviated as C6B).

Working a front cable

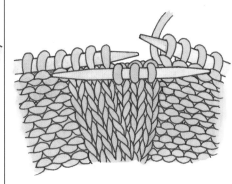

1 Slip the first three stitches of the group purlwise onto a cable needle and hold them at the front of the work.

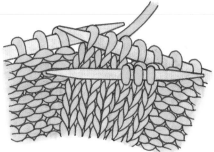

2 Keep the stitches held at the front in the center of the cable needle to prevent them from slipping off, and knit the next three stitches on the left needle.

3 Knit the three stitches in turn from the cable needle. If you find this awkward, return the stitches to the left needle before knitting them.

Working a back cable

1 Slip the first three stitches of the group purlwise onto a cable needle and hold them at the back of the work.

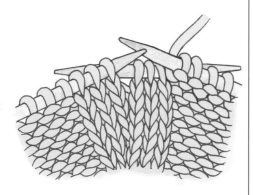

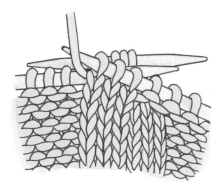

2 Keep the stitches held at the back in the center of the cable needle to prevent them from slipping off, and knit the next three stitches on the left needle.

3 Knit the three stitches in turn from the cable needle. If you find this awkward, return the stitches to the left needle before knitting them.

Working yarn overs

A yarn over is a decorative increase used when working lace patterns, and to increase a stitch at the beginning of a row when working diagonally. It is made by wrapping the yarn around the right needle in various ways, depending on where the yarn over is placed in the instructions.

1 To work a yarn over between two knit stitches, bring the yarn between the needles from the back to the front of the work. Knit the next stitch, taking the yarn to the back over the right needle.

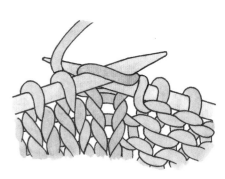

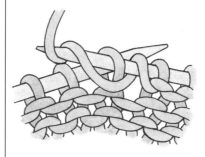

2 To work a yarn over between a knit and a purl stitch, bring the yarn between the needles from the back to the front. Take it back over the right needle and then to the front again. Purl the next stitch.

3 To work a yarn over between a purl and a knit stitch, leave the yarn at the front of the work. Knit the next stitch, taking the yarn to the back over the right needle.

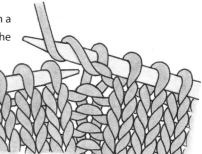

4 To work a yarn over between two purl stitches, leave the yarn at the front of the work. Take it to the back over the right needle and then to the front again. Purl the next stitch.

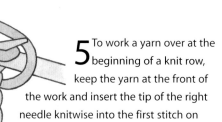

5 To work a yarn over at the beginning of a knit row, keep the yarn at the front of the work and insert the tip of the right needle knitwise into the first stitch on the left needle. Take the yarn to the back over the right needle and knit the stitch.

6 To work a yarn over at the beginning of a purl row, keep the yarn at the back of the work and insert the tip of the right needle purlwise into the first stitch on the left needle. Take the yarn to the front over the right needle and purl the stitch.

Techniques for multicolored knitting

Multicolored knitting patterns are usually worked from a chart. The chart shows the pattern as a series of colored squares and each square represents one stitch. Two-color patterns (also known as jacquard and Fair Isle knitting) have small, repeating areas of color. Two yarns are used to work each row, with the color not in use carried across the wrong side of the work, so producing a double-thickness fabric.

Intarsia patterns have larger areas of color. Any number of colors may be used in a row, and each color is worked with a separate length of yarn. The yarn is not carried across the wrong side of the work, and so a single-thickness fabric is produced.

Reading a chart

Read a two-color or intarsia chart in the same way. Start at the bottom right-hand corner of the chart, and work the pattern row by row. Each square on the chart represents one stitch. Always work upwards from the bottom of the chart, reading odd-numbered rows (right-side rows: knit all the stitches from right to left and even-numbered rows (wrong-side rows: purl all the stitches) from left to right.

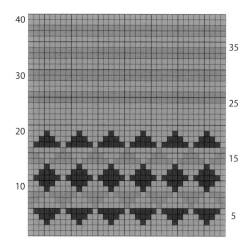

Two-color knitting

When changing colors as they appear on the chart, carry the yarn not in use loosely across the wrong side of the work and pick it up again when it is needed. This is called "stranding," and it works well when there are small areas of color repeated along a row.

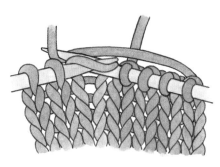

1 On knit (right-side) rows, knit the first group of stitches in the first color, then let the yarn drop. Bring the new color over the top of the dropped yarn and knit along the row to the next group on the chart in the first color.

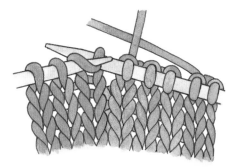

2 Let the second yarn drop, bring the first color under the dropped yarn and knit to the next group in the second color. Repeat along the row.

3 On purl (wrong-side) rows, purl the first group of stitches in the first color, then let the yarn drop. Bring the new color over the top of the dropped yarn and purl along the row to the next group on the chart in the first color.

4 Let the second yarn drop, bring the first color under the dropped yarn and purl to the next group in the second color. Repeat along the row.

Intarsia knitting

Use the intarsia technique when the design is formed of solid areas of color. The yarns are not stranded across the back of the work, but a separate length is used to work each area. Prevent the yarn from tangling by winding it into several small balls, or by winding it onto plastic bobbins. To stop holes forming where color areas meet, twist the yarns around each other at each color change as shown.

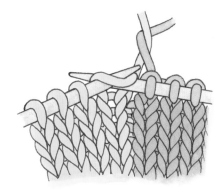

1 To change color on a knit (right-side) row, drop the old color. Pick up the new color from beneath the old color and knit along the row to the next color change.

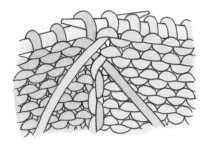

2 To change color on a purl (wrong-side) row, drop the old color. Pick up the new color from beneath the old color and purl along the row to the next color change.

Decorative techniques

Bobbles and beads add textural and visual interest to the surface of a knitted block. A bobble is a three-dimensional stitch that stands out from the background. Each bobble is made over several rows by increasing several times into the same stitch, working one or more rows straight and then decreasing back to one stitch. Beads are threaded onto the main yarn before casting on, then are knitted into the fabric one by one as they appear in the pattern instructions.

Working bobbles

Bobbles are often worked with the main yarn, but bobbles worked in a contrasting color need a separate length of yarn for each one. There are several methods of making bobbles, but they all follow a sequence similar to the five-stitch bobble shown here.

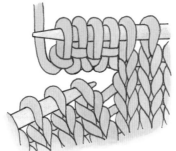

1 Make five stitches into the same stitch by knitting into the front and back of the stitch twice without slipping it off the needle. Then knit into the front of the stitch once more and slip the original stitch off the needle.

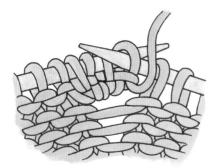

2 Turn the work. Purl the five stitches made on the previous row, turn, then knit the five stitches. This sequence may be repeated when making a large bobble.

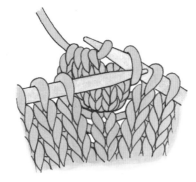

3 To complete the bobble, use the tip of the left needle to lift the second, third, fourth, and fifth stitches, one at a time, over the first stitch and off the needle.

Applying beads

Choose beads with a hole that is large enough to allow the beads to be threaded onto the yarn and slipped along easily without snagging. Thread all the beads required for the pattern before casting on. When using more than one bead color, take care to thread the beads onto the yarn in the correct sequence.

1 Knit along the row to the position of the bead. Bring the yarn and the first bead to the front of the work. Slip the next stitch purlwise onto the right needle.

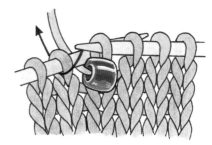

2 Slide the bead down the yarn until it rests snugly against the work, then take the yarn to the back and knit the next stitch in the usual way. Repeat as required.

Blocking

Blocking is the process of ensuring that a piece of knitting is the correct size and shape. It involves pinning out a knitted piece to the correct size then, depending on the fiber content of the yarn, either steaming it with an iron or moistening it with cold water.

Block woolen yarns by holding a steam iron (set at the correct temperature for the yarn) about $\frac{3}{4}$ in. (2cm) above the block. Let the steam penetrate for several seconds without allowing the iron to come into contact with the wool. To block cotton, acrylic, and blended yarns, pin out the pieces and then use a spray bottle to mist the block with cold water until it is evenly moist all over, but not saturated. Do not use the iron.

1 Pin out several blocks on your ironing board (or use a specialist blocking board) using rustproof pins, and ease each block into shape.

2 Block as above. Allow the blocks to dry before removing the pins.

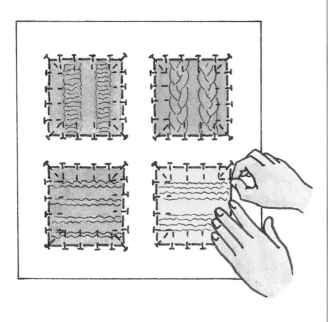

Joining blocks

Block each knitted piece before joining. Use matching yarn, threaded in a tapestry needle, to sew the blocks together. Lay out the blocks in the correct order. Join each vertical or horizontal row of blocks to make a long strip, using one of the methods shown, then join the strips together.

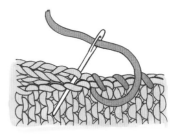

1 To join blocks with mattress stitch, stitch with the right sides of the blocks facing upward. Using a tapestry needle and matching yarn, weave around the centers of the stitches as shown. Join row ends in the same way.

2 To join blocks by overcasting, hold two blocks together with their right sides facing, pinning if necessary. Work a row of diagonal stitches (from back to front) through the strands at the edges of the blocks.

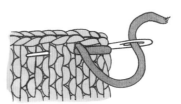

3 To begin a backstitch seam, hold two blocks together with their right sides facing, pinning if necessary. Secure the end of the seam by taking the needle twice around the edges from front to back. Bring the needle out a short distance away.

4 Insert the needle at the point where the yarn emerges from the previous stitch and bring it out a short distance in front. Pull the yarn through to complete the stitch and repeat along the edge.

Knitting an edging

Afghans can be trimmed with various types of edging. The edgings shown here are worked in rows across the width of the strip, so you can make them any length by simply repeating the pattern as many times as you require. Make the strip long enough to go right around the afghan; also allow extra to be gathered or pleated around the corners, so the edging will lie flat when it is attached. Pin the edging in place and stitch with matching yarn.

Straight Edging

CO 11 sts.
ROW 1: (RS) K2, P2, K1, YO, K2tog, P2, K2.
ROW 2: K4, P3, K4.
ROW 3: Knit.
ROW 4: K2, P7, K2.
Rep Rows 1–4 for required length, ending with a Row 4.
BO.

Zigzag Edging

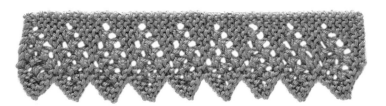

CO 8 sts and K one row.
ROW 1: (WS) Sl 1, K1, [YO, K2tog] twice, YO, K2.
ROW 2 AND EVERY ALT ROW: Sl 1, K to end.
ROW 3: Sl 1, K2, [YO, K2tog] twice, YO, K2.
ROW 5: Sl 1, K3, [YO, K2tog] twice, YO, K2.
ROW 7: Sl 1, K4, [YO, K2tog] twice, YO, K2.
ROW 9: Sl 1, K to end.
ROW 10: BO 4 sts, K to end.
Rep Rows 1–10 for required length, ending with a Row 10.
BO.

Sawtooth Edging

CO 8 sts and K 1 row.

ROW 1: (WS) Sl 1, K1, [YO, K2tog] twice, YO, K2.

ROW 2: K2, YO, K2, [YO, K2tog] twice, K1.

ROW 3: Sl 1, K1, [YO, K2tog] twice, K2, YO, K2.

ROW 4: K2, YO, K4, [YO, K2tog] twice, K1.

ROW 5: Sl 1, K1, [YO, K2tog] twice, K4, YO, K2.

ROW 6: K2, YO, K6, [YO, K2tog] twice, K1.

ROW 7: Sl 1, K1, [YO, K2tog] twice, K6, YO, K2.

ROW 8: K2, YO, K8, [YO, K2tog] twice, K1.

ROW 9: Sl 1, K1, [YO, K2tog] twice, K8, YO, K2.

ROW 10: K2, YO, K10, [YO, K2tog] twice, K1.

ROW 11: Sl 1, K1, [YO, K2tog] twice, K10, YO, K2.

ROW 12: BO 11 sts, K2, [YO, K2tog] twice, K1.

Rep Rows 1–12 for required length, ending with a Row 12. BO.

Leaf Edging

Special abbreviation

INC = increase by knitting into the front and back of next stitch.

CO 8 sts.

ROW 1: K5, YO, K1, YO, K2.

ROW 2: P6, inc, K3.

ROW 3: K4, P1, K2, YO, K1, YO, K3.

ROW 4: P8, inc, K4.

ROW 5: K4, P2, K3, YO, K1, YO, K4.

ROW 6: P10, inc, K5.

ROW 7: K4, P3, K4, YO, K1, YO, K5.

ROW 8: P12, inc, K6.

ROW 9: K4, P4, sl 1, K1, psso, K7, K2tog, K1.

ROW 10: P10, inc, K7.

ROW 11: K4, P5, sl 1, K1, psso, K5, K2tog, K1.

ROW 12: P8, inc, K2, P1, K5.

ROW 13: K4, P1, K1, P4, sl 1, K1, psso, K3, K2tog, K1.

ROW 14: P6, inc, K3, P1, K5.

ROW 15: K4, P1, K1, P5, sl 1, K1, psso, K1, K2tog, K1.

ROW 16: P4, inc, K4, P1, K5.

ROW 17: K4, P1, K1, P6, sl 1, K2tog, psso, K1.

ROW 18: P2tog, BO next 5 sts using P2tog st when BO first st, P3, K4.

Rep Rows 1–18 for required length, ending with a Row 18. BO.

Curly Fringe

CO 20 sts.
ROW 1: (RS) BO 15 sts, K4.
ROW 2: K5.
ROW 3: CO 15 sts.

Rep Rows 1–3 for required length, ending with a Row 1.
BO.

Ruffled Edging

CO 12 sts.
ROW 1: (WS) Knit.
ROW 2: P9, turn, K9.
ROW 3: P9, K3.
ROW 4: K3, P9.

ROW 5: K9, turn, P9.
ROW 6: Knit.
Rep Rows 1–6 for required length, ending with a Row 6.
BO.

Care of afghans

Knitted afghans look wonderful used as throws for a chair or couch, and they add warmth as well as decoration to any room. An afghan worked in bright, lively colors can spruce up plain, neutral decor; afghans can also be designed to blend into the decor of a room by matching the colors to the room's decorative scheme. Mini afghans make popular gifts for babies, and can be used as crib covers or shawls.

Always clean your afghan regularly, whether it's being used or displayed. Be guided by the care instructions on the yarn and clean accordingly. If the afghan is very large, you may prefer to have it professionally dry-cleaned.

When storing afghans that are not in use, don't enclose them in a polythene bag as the yarn fibers will not be able to breathe and the static cling created by polythene will attract dust and dirt to your knitting. Instead, wrap the afghan in a clean cotton pillowcase or sheet. Store this in a dry, cool, dust-free place (ideally a linen chest or chest of drawers), adding a bag of dried lavender to keep the knitting smelling sweet and to deter moths.

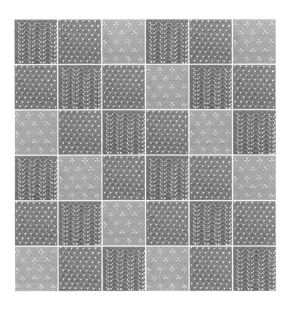

Yarn list

When creating the blocks in this book, colors were chosen from a wide palette of almost ninety shades of pure wool double knitting (DK weight) yarn. Here's a list of the actual yarns used, arranged by color.

white King Cole Merino DK, shade 'Snow White' (blocks 29, 57, 60, 104, 200)

cream Jaeger Matchmaker DK, shade 662 (blocks 102, 148, 185, 191)

light natural Jaeger Matchmaker DK, shade 663 (blocks 38, 82, 104, 108, 110, 114, 147, 152, 153, 195)

oatmeal Jaeger Extra Fine Merino DK, shade 936 (blocks 31, 130, 177)

acid lemon Jaeger Matchmaker DK, shade 895 (blocks 34, 66, 100, 103, 112, 116, 156, 167, 192)

butter Jaeger Matchmaker DK, shade 727 (blocks 11, 30, 44, 61, 68, 93, 138, 144, 148, 205, 209)

sunshine yellow King Cole Merino DK, shade 'Gold' (blocks 10, 46, 47, 71, 77, 80, 87, 103, 117, 128, 132, 139, 168, 172, 207, 211)

amber King Cole Merino DK, shade 'Amber' (blocks 11, 30, 38, 44, 64, 68, 77, 79, 94, 149, 155, 168, 209)

sand King Cole Merino DK, shade 'Sand' (blocks 26, 41, 127, 152, 156, 163, 181, 185)

camel Debbie Bliss Merino DK, shade 103 (blocks 38, 117, 121, 131, 152, 156, 163)

soft camel Jaeger Matchmaker DK, shade 865 (blocks 96)

orange Jaeger Matchmaker DK, shade 898 (blocks 2, 46, 48, 103, 117, 133, 137, 155, 168, 172, 173, 177, 186)

copper King Cole Merino DK, shade 'Copper' (blocks 63, 94, 196)

burnt orange Jaeger Extra Fine Merino DK, shade 979 (blocks 4, 11, 77, 78, 96, 145, 151, 191)

rust Jaeger Matchmaker DK, shade 901 (blocks 32, 149, 205, 209)

salmon King Cole Merino DK, shade 'Salmon' (blocks 25, 26, 86, 98)

pale coral Jaeger Matchmaker DK, shade 881 (blocks 26, 27, 50, 88, 102, 106, 130, 161)

bright coral King Cole Merino DK, shade 'Coral' (block 161)

dark coral Jaeger Matchmaker DK, shade 870 (blocks 26, 28, 52, 85, 102, 126, 130, 157, 161)

scarlet King Cole Merino DK, shade 'Scarlet' 132, (block 132, 155)

cherry Debbie Bliss Merino DK, shade 700 (blocks 9, 45, 47, 57, 58, 60, 120, 124, 132, 151)

wineberry Jaeger Extra Fine Merino DK, shade 920 (blocks 12, 77, 148, 167, 171)

claret Jaeger Matchmaker DK, shade 656 (blocks 175, 179, 184, 188, 210)

dark raspberry Jaeger Extra Fine Merino DK, shade 943 (blocks 141, 145, 151, 155, 165)

burgundy Jaeger Matchmaker DK, shade 655 (blocks 9, 45, 47, 167, 171, 179, 206)

elderberry Jaeger Extra Fine Merino DK, shade 944 (blocks 18, 20, 120, 151)

rose petal Jaeger Extra Fine Merino DK, shade 982 (blocks 20, 113, 157, 161)

baby pink Jaeger Baby Merino DK shade 221 (blocks 55, 109)

variegated pale pink Jaeger Baby Merino DK, shade 212 (blocks 53, 97, 113, 143, 147, 175, 179, 210)

pale violet Jaeger Matchmaker DK, shade 893 (blocks 13, 53, 91, 166)

dawn pink Jaeger Matchmaker DK, shade 883 (blocks 45, 54, 113, 119, 123, 156)

cupid pink Jaeger Extra Fine Merino DK, shade 989 (block 15)

clover pink King Cole Merino DK, shade 'Dusky Pink' (blocks 17, 88, 98, 113, 193, 206, 210)

fuchsia Jaeger Matchmaker DK, shade 896 (blocks 34, 54, 71, 86, 88, 115, 120, 128, 132, 155, 160, 164, 189, 203)

light raspberry King Cole Merino DK, shade 'Raspberry' (blocks 20, 33, 34, 36, 72, 87, 88, 98, 104, 111, 115, 174, 178, 199, 210)

variegated fuchsia Jaeger Baby Merino DK, shade 193 (blocks 56, 104, 147)

magenta Jaeger Matchmaker DK, shade 887 (blocks 19, 88, 98, 115, 120, 132, 155, 165, 169)

hydrangea Jaeger Extra Fine Merino DK, shade 992 (blocks 18, 20)

aubergine Jaeger Matchmaker DK, shade 894 (blocks 15, 20, 109, 113, 153)

pearl Jaeger Matchmaker DK, shade 891 (blocks 15, 166, 170, 201, 212)

mauve Jaeger Matchmaker DK, shade 882 (blocks 15, 56, 84, 91, 102, 125, 129, 150, 156, 178, 183, 187, 197, 201)

deep mauve King Cole Merino DK, shade 'Mauve' (blocks 14, 91, 136, 140, 164, 174, 178)

loganberry Jaeger Extra Fine Merino DK, shade 991 (blocks 15, 34, 35, 82, 92)

antique violet Jaeger Matchmaker DK, shade 626 (blocks 15, 153, 212)

lavender Jaeger Matchmaker DK, shade 888 (blocks 16, 34, 73, 76, 90, 91, 92, 111, 115, 129, 160, 164, 166, 208, 212)

amethyst Jaeger Matchmaker DK, shade 897 (blocks 70, 115, 125, 129, 141, 145, 189, 212)

variegated purple Jaeger Baby Merino DK, shade 194 (blocks 89, 166, 170)

African violet King Cole Merino DK, shade 'African Violet' (blocks 14, 89, 129, 140, 165, 197)

putty Jaeger Matchmaker DK, shade 892 (blocks 7, 8, 37, 154, 158, 162)

variegated pale blue Jaeger Baby Merino DK, shade 213 (blocks 5, 7, 143, 147)

sky blue Jaeger Matchmaker DK, shade 864 (blocks 6, 99, 176, 180, 187)

powder blue Debbie Bliss Merino DK, shade 213 (blocks 81, 190, 194)

ocean blue Jaeger Extra Fine Merino DK, shade 940 (blocks 26, 41, 150, 154)

bluebell King Cole Merino DK, shade 'Bluebell' (blocks 5, 7, 71, 84, 101, 105, 119, 145, 164, 176, 180, 190)

larkspur King Cole Merino DK, shade 'Larkspur' (blocks 43, 44, 69, 83, 150, 154, 167, 199, 203)

slate blue King Cole Merino DK, shade 'Slate Blue' (blocks 3, 194, 198, 202)

mariner blue Jaeger Matchmaker DK, shade 629 (blocks 1, 4, 101, 129, 150, 154)

blackcurrant Jaeger Extra Fine Merino DK, shade 945 (blocks 7, 150)

pale turquoise Jaeger Matchmaker DK, shade 884 (blocks 24, 74, 84, 100, 101, 112, 116, 119, 123, 130, 135, 154, 156, 162, 211)

medium turquoise King Cole Merino DK, shade 'Turquoise' (blocks 23, 49, 73, 101, 116, 119, 189, 211)

variegated turquoise Jaeger Baby Merino DK, shade 192 (blocks 52, 126, 139, 193, 207)

Marina blue Jaeger Extra Fine Merino DK, shade 986 (blocks 1, 4, 21, 76, 82, 130, 162, 165, 169, 208)

Capri blue Debbie Bliss Merino DK, shade 202 (blocks 21, 44, 45, 76, 116, 124, 154, 158, 162, 188, 211)

bright jade King Cole Merino DK, shade 'Green Ice' (blocks 21, 34, 36, 69)

emerald King Cole Merino DK, shade 'Emerald' (blocks 57, 59)

balm Jaeger Extra Fine Merino DK, shade 990 (blocks 21, 65, 118, 122, 183, 187)

grass green Cygnet Superwash DK, shade 2817 (blocks 41, 44, 68, 118, 142, 146)

linden green King Cole Merino DK, shade 'Linden' (blocks 14, 26, 28)

lime Debbie Bliss Merino DK, shade 503 (blocks 1, 2, 4, 146, 182, 186, 192, 196)

hop Jaeger Matchmaker DK, shade 899 (blocks 21, 22, 42, 116, 118, 149, 204)

sage green Jaeger Matchmaker DK, shade 857 (blocks 24, 103, 107, 149, 153)

bottle green King Cole Merino DK, shade 'Bottle Green' (blocks 21, 44, 66, 118, 122)

bright olive Debbie Bliss Merino DK, shade 502 (blocks 146, 192)

dull olive King Cole Merino DK, shade 'Olive' (block 67)

loden Jaeger Matchmaker DK, shade 730 (blocks 142, 146)

variegated green Jaeger Baby Merino DK, shade 191 (blocks 198, 202)

dark natural Jaeger Extra Fine Merino DK, shade 937 (blocks 40, 45, 152)

mushroom Jaeger Matchmaker DK, shade 880 (blocks 29, 62, 114, 149, 200, 204)

mocha Jaeger Matchmaker DK, shade 900 (blocks 64, 114, 134, 138, 173, 177, 182, 186)

brown marl Jaeger Extra Fine Merino DK, shade 975 (blocks 30, 63, 168)

mink King Cole Merino DK, shade 'Mink' (blocks 95, 131, 209)

cocoa Jaeger Extra Fine Merino DK, shade 972 (blocks 127, 131, 190, 195)

cirrus Jaeger Extra Fine Merino DK, shade 981 (block 131)

silver gray King Cole Merino DK, shade 'Silver' (blocks 38, 75, 152, 153)

ash Jaeger Extra Fine Merino DK, shade 976 (blocks 32, 39, 73, 114, 117, 121)

flannel gray Jaeger Matchmaker DK, shade 782 (blocks 51, 110, 114, 131, 181, 185, 191)

granite Jaeger Matchmaker DK, shade 639 (blocks 38, 76, 137)

badger marl Jaeger Extra Fine Merino DK, shade 977 (blocks 30, 153, 159, 163, 184, 188)

charcoal Jaeger Extra Fine Merino DK, shade 959 (blocks 20, 39, 76, 77, 80, 144, 148, 159, 163, 180)

INDEX

A abbreviations 111
Abstract 44
afghans, care of 125
Allsorts 46
Arrowheads 55

B beads, to apply 121
Beads, Alternate 81
Bee Stitch 82
Big Cross 106
binding off 114
Block Checkers 55
blocking 122
blocks, to join 122
Blocks, Little 33
  Ridged 41
Blocky 68
Blue Seas 80
bobbles 121
Bobbles, Colorful 51
  Random 90
Bricks 89
Button Up 77
Buzz 69

C Cable(s): Arched 53
  Classic 77
  Double 43
  Interlaced 64
  Little 48
  and Rib 51
  Surface 35
cables 117–118
Candy Cane 59
casting on 112
Chain Gang 75
Checks 71
Chevron(s) 63

Eyelets 70
Lace 32
color chart, to read 119
color palette 15
colors 14
Columns, Ridged 69
  Zigzag 65
Counterpoint 101
Crisscross 85
Crystal Sparkle 54

D Dash 70
decreases 116–117
Deepdale 49
designing 16–17
designs: Baby Lace 27
  Blue Geometric 20
  Bobble Fantasy 19
  Bright and Bold 24
  Buttoned Pillow 26
  Edwardian
    Counterpane 23
  Heart's Delight 18
  Holiday Pillow 26
  Merry-Go-Round 22
  Modern Times 21
  Nocturne 25
Diamond(s) 74
  Beaded 88
  Seeded 45
Dolly Mixtures 65

E edgings 123–125
Eyelets 47
  Alternate 66
  Chevron 70
  Diamond 76
  Double 31
  Zigzag 41

F Flapover 43

Flowers, Little 78
Flowing Pinks 38
frame 17
Furrows 97

G gauge 114

H Harris 104
Heart, Big 57
  Reversed 38
Honeycomb 72
Humbug 44

I increases 116
intarsia knitting 120
Interwoven 60

J Jacob's Ladder 86

K Knots, Little 39

L Lattice 68
Leaf/Leaves: Banded 48
  Beaded 71
  Elsie's Rose 60
  Fall 92
  Lace 46
  Plain 40
  Scattered 78
  Solid 100
Light and Shade 75

M Mirror Image 37
Mock Houndstooth 47
Morse Code 49
Mosaic 79

N needles 111

O Offset 30
On Point 52

Patch 99
patterns: diamond 17
  sawtooth 16
  stepped zigzag 17
  stripes 17
  windmill 16

P Piazza 72
Pink Flashes 56
Pinstripes 34
Plain and Fancy 74
Polperro 57
Purple Haze 87
Pyramids 61

R Ribby 36
Ridges 103
  Horizontal 34
Ritzy 35
River 50
row below, to knit into 115

S St. Ives 54
sample swatch 110, 111
Sextet 42
Shady Ladders 39
Shutter 73
slip knot 112
Snowflake Lace 58
Softie 79
Speckle 30
Speckled Bands 93
Square(s): Beaded 62
  Corner 91
  Four 96
  Framed 56
  Seed 67
Staircase 50
stitches 113
  to slip 115
  to work into back of 115

Stripe(s): Bobble 84
  Eccentric 67
  Holiday 58
  Hot 73
  Indian 63
  Linked 52
  Loop 45
  Mini 32
  Oblique 102
  Soft 95
  Toffee 61
  V- 105
  Vertical 62
  Waffle 98
Striped Basketweave 83

T Tabard 40
Tango 53
Target 33
texture 15
Threaded Ribbons 31
Toronto 76
Tree, Beaded 59
Troika 36
Twilight 37
Twin Triangles 64
two-color knitting 120
Two Edges 66

U Up and Over 94

W Waves, Little 107
Wavy Ribbons 42

Y yarn 110–111, 126–127
  amounts 110
  to join 114
yarn overs 118–119

SUPPLIERS

AMERICAN SUPPLIERS
Cygnet Yarns
Available from
www.mcadirect.com

Debbie Bliss Yarns
Knitting Fever, Inc.
35 Debevoise Avenue
Roosevelt, NY 11575
www.knittingfever.com

Jaeger Yarns
Westminster Fibers
4 Townsend West, Unit 8
Nashua, NH 03063

King Cole
Cascade Yarns
PO Box 58168
Tukwila, WA 98188
www.cascadeyarns.com

Rowan
Westminster Fibers
4 Townsend West, Unit 8
Nashua, NH 03063
www.knitrowan.com

CANADIAN SUPPLIERS
Diamond Yarn
St. Laurent, Ste. 101
Montreal, QC H3L 2N1
www.diamondyarn.com

ACKNOWLEDGMENTS

Jan Eaton would like to thank Jaeger Handknits for supplying yarns to knit many of the blocks.

All photos and illustrations are the copyright of Quarto Publishing plc.

While every effort has been made to credit contributors, Quarto would like to apologize should there have been any omissions or errors—and would be pleased to make the appropriate correction for future editions of the book.